CURING FORGETFULNESS

A Translation of *al-Kashf wa al-Bayān fī mā Yataʿallaq bi an-Nisyān* & *ʿIlāj an-Nisyān*

Sheikh ʿAbd al-Ghanī ibn Ismāʿīl al-Nābulsī

Ḥabīb Muhammad ibn ʿAlawī al-ʿAydarūs

Translated by

Talut ibn Sulaiman Dawood

TITLE: CURING FORGETFULNESS
ISBN: 978-1-952306-79-2

FIRST EDITION | AUGUST 2024

AUTHORS: SHEIKH ABD AL-GHANI IBN ISMAIL AL-NABLUSI
AND HABIB MUHAMMAD IBN ALAWI AL-AYDARUS

TYPESETTING: IGP CONSULTING | WWW.IGPCONSULTING.COM
DISTRIBUTION: WWW.SATTAURPUBLISHING.COM

CONTENTS

PUBLISHER'S MESSAGE vii

THE AUTHORS ix

BOOK ONE:
REVELATION AND CLARIFICATION OF WHAT CONCERNS FORGETFULNESS

Editor's Introduction 4

Author's Preface 8

Chapter 1: On the Meaning of Forgetfulness 14

Chapter 2: An Explanation of the Causes of Forgetfulness and a Clarification of the Meaning of This Ailment Which Amounts to Absent-Mindedness and Negligence 20

Chapter 3: A Mention of the Treatments for Memorization Which Requires the Removal of Forgetfulness and the Elimination of This Illness from Certain Verses of the Qur'an and Prophetic Ḥadīths and Statements of the Righteous Elect, Which the Scholars Have Tried and Tested and Mentioned in Their Books 22

Chapter 4 - Treatments Used for Memory Retention 40

Chapter 5 - On Legal Rulings 46

Epilogue 52

BOOK TWO:
THE CURE FOR FORGETFULNESS

Introduction 66

Verses and Supplications That Treat Forgetfulness and Assist in Memorization 68

The Prayer for Memorization of the Qur'an and Its Supplication 78

A Supplication for Memorizing the Qur'an 82

Various Beneficial Formulas 84

Herbs and Foods That Help One to Memorize and Avoid Forgetfulness 96

Some Compounds That Strengthen One's Retention and Assist in Memorization 98

الحمد لله

توكلت على الله

Publisher's Message

In the name of Allah, the Most Merciful and the Compassionate

All praise and gratitude is due to Allah, our Most Generous and Merciful Benefactor. He infinitely bestows His divine grace upon us and has distinguished us all by making us members of the esteemed Ummah of our master Muhammad ﷺ.

I bear witness that there is no being or deity worthy of worship except Allah, and that our master Muhammad ﷺ is His last and final Messenger.

O Allah, send blessings and bounties upon our master Muhammad, the opener of what was once deemed inaccessible, the seal of what had preceded, the helper of the truth by the Truth, and the guide to Your straight path. May He send prayers upon his pure and noble family commensurate to his greatness and magnificent rank.

This compilation of two treatises, *al-Kashf wa al-Bayān fī mā Yataʿallaq bi al-Nisyān & ʿIlāj al-Nisyān*, one from the classical era and one from the 20th century, contains both conceptual discussion and practical advice on how to address the universal issue of overcoming forgetfulness and strengthening memory.

Although focused on a very specific topic, the benefits of this text are numerous and comprehensive, since memory and cognitive retention affect so many aspects of our lives. Thus, even if one implements only a few of its recommendations, this is a book that is sure to prove useful and bring long term blessings to one's life.

Curing Forgetfulness delves into the multifaceted nature of forgetfulness, exploring its spiritual and physical dimensions. Both authors share their thoughts on the meaning of forgetfulness, drawing from Qur'anic verses and Prophetic traditions. The authors then provide a detailed analysis of the causes of forgetfulness, identifying both physical and spiritual factors. This comprehensive approach highlights the holistic nature of our tradition, which address the well-being of both body and soul.

One of the book's most significant contributions is its discussion on remedies and treatments for forgetfulness. The authors offer a range of solutions, from spiritual practices like prayer and recitation of specific Qur'anic verses to practical advice on diet and lifestyle. They emphasize the importance of a balanced approach, combining spiritual discipline with physical care to achieve optimal memory and mental clarity. This reflects the broader Islamic ethos of balance and moderation in all aspects of life.

The book also explores the ethical and legal dimensions of forgetfulness, particularly concerning religious obligations. The authors provide guidance on how to navigate forgetfulness in the context of worship and daily life, offering a compassionate and understanding perspective.

On behalf of the entire publishing team, I publicly thank every member of Imam Ghazali Publishing's reading community. We extend our sincere gratitude to all members who have supported this project, including our translators, editors, proofreaders, and the entire team at IGP.

Anything undignified in this rendering is from our own souls and ignorance, and anything herein which is of benefit is solely from Allah, the blessings of the authors, and the scholars who worked hard to preserve, transmit, and save these blessed and noble works. May Allah forgive us for our inadequacies, and may He bless all those who teach, read, and study the entirety or portion of this work until the Day of Judgement. I end by asking that should you, that is, the reader, benefit from this text, then kindly remember this poor and needy servant and his family in your supplications.

Āmīn. And all praise is due to Allah, Lord of the worlds.

– Muhammad Adnaan Sattaur (Abu Fārīs)
On behalf of Imam Ghazali Publishing

The Authors

Sheikh ʿAbd al-Ghan ibn Ismāʿīl al-Nābulsī (1641 – 1731), was an eminent scholar and poet of Ottoman Damascus. The Sheikh's family included many scholars and judges of the lands of Shām and Egypt during both the Mamluk and Ottoman eras, and included many eminent scholars whose works are known down to the present day. He authored over 200 works on a wide range of subjects, and passed away in Damascus at 90 years of age.

Ḥabīb Muhammad ibn ʿAlawī al-ʿAydarūs, born in 1932 in Tarim, hailed from a distinguished lineage tracing back to Prophet Muhammad ﷺ. Raised in a scholarly and pious environment, he studied under numerous eminent scholars. His life was marked by dedication to Islamic knowledge and spiritual guidance, even enduring three and a half years of severe torture in prison under a socialist regime. He authored over one hundred concise and beneficial books on various Islamic topics. Known for his open hospitality and compassionate heart, he supported students of knowledge and emphasized respect for sacred texts. He passed away on October 6, 2011, leaving behind a legacy of scholarship and spiritual leadership.

Book One

الكِتَابُ الأَوَّلُ

REVELATION AND CLARIFICATION OF WHAT CONCERNS FORGETFULNESS

SHEIKH ʿABD AL-GHANĪ IBN ISMĀʿĪL AL-NĀBULSĪ

رِسَالَةُ
الْكَشْفِ وَالْبَيَانِ
فِيمَا يَتَعَلَّقُ بِالنِّسْيَانِ

عَبْدِ الْغَنِيِّ بْنِ إِسْمَاعِيلَ النَّابُلُسِيُّ

In the Name of Allah, the Most Beneficent, the Most Merciful

Editor's Introduction

All praise is due to Allah, Who created human beings from dust, distributed among them gifts and intellects, and revealed to His saints what had been hidden and concealed from others. He then brought before them the door of the path that leads to goodness.

Pursuant to the famous adage, "Necessity is the mother of invention," I began to research and meditate, which is in fact something that the Noble Qur'an has encouraged, as found in His ﷻ words: "Those who remember Allah while standing, sitting, and lying on their sides and reflect on the creation of the Heavens and the Earth."[10] Every craftsman in their field of expertise employs rules and regulations to ensure the preservation of their skill domain, whether it be a vehicle or a machine. As such, it is even more the case that this great Creator, Who fashioned humanity in the best form, established rules and regulations for them, thereby providing them with safety and security.

However, it does not befit a rational being to know the true path of guidance and then deviate from it. Such people are those against whom the words of Allah have been revealed and proven true: "But most of the people do not know. They know what is apparent of the worldly life, but they, of the Hereafter, are unaware."[11] This process of contemplation led me to probe the books of knowledge. During my investigation of historical manuscripts, I found this treatise, entitled *al-Kashf wa al-Bayān*, which relieved me of distress and brought the path of spiritual enlightenment and self-discovery closer. The one that directs to goodness is like the one who practices it.

---

10 *Āl 'Imrān*, 191.

11 *al-Rūm*, 7-8.

بِسْمِ اللهِ الرَّحْمَنِ الرَّحِيمِ

مُقَدِّمَةٌ

الْحَمْدُ للهِ الَّذِي خَلَقَ الْخَلْقَ مِنْ تُرَابٍ وَفَرَّقَ بَيْنَهُمْ فِي الْمَعَادِنِ وَالْأَلْبَابِ وَكَشَفَ لِأَوْلِيَائِهِ مَا خَفِيَ عَنْ غَيْرِهِمْ وَغَابَ، فَجَعَلَهُمْ فِي سَبِيلِ الْهِدَايَةِ إِلَى الْخَيْرِ عَلَى الْبَابِ، وَطِبْقًا لِلْقَاعِدَةِ الْمَشْهُورَةِ: الْحَاجَةُ أُمُّ الِاخْتِرَاعِ، جَعَلَتْنِي أَبْحَثُ وَأَتَفَكَّرُ، فَالْقُرْآنُ الْكَرِيمُ حَثَّ عَلَى ذَلِكَ فِي قَوْلِهِ تَعَالَى: الَّذِينَ يَذْكُرُونَ اللَّهَ قِيَامًا وَقُعُودًا وَعَلَى جُنُوبِهِمْ وَيَتَفَكَّرُونَ فِي خَلْقِ السَّمَوَاتِ وَالْأَرْضِ[1]. إِنَّ كُلَّ صَانِعٍ يَصْنَعُ لِصَنْعَتِهِ الْقَوَاعِدَ وَالضَّوَابِطَ الَّتِي تَكْفُلُ لَهَا صِيَانَتَهَا سَوَاءٌ أَكَانَتْ هَذِهِ سَيَّارَةً أَمْ مَاكِينَةً، وَمِنْ بَابِ أَوْلَى هَذَا الْخَالِقُ الْعَظِيمُ الَّذِي خَلَقَ الْإِنْسَانَ فِي أَحْسَنِ تَقْوِيمٍ، جَعَلَ لَهُ الْقَوَاعِدَ وَالضَّوَابِطَ الَّتِي تُوَفِّرُ لَهُ السَّلَامَةَ وَالْأَمَانَ، وَلَكِنْ لَيْسَ بِعَاقِلٍ مَنْ عَرَفَ السَّبِيلَ ثُمَّ حَادَ، وَلَكِنْ حَقَّ عَلَيْهِمْ قَوْلُهُ تَعَالَى ﴿وَلَٰكِنَّ أَكْثَرَ النَّاسِ لَا يَعْلَمُونَ ۝ يَعْلَمُونَ ظَاهِرًا مِّنَ الْحَيَاةِ الدُّنْيَا وَهُمْ عَنِ الْآخِرَةِ هُمْ غَافِلُونَ﴾[2] وَهَذَا مَا جَعَلَنِي أَبْحَثُ فِي كُتُبِ الْعِلْمِ. وَأَثْنَاءَ بَحْثِي فِي كُتُبِ التُّرَاثِ لَا سِيَمَا الْكُتُبِ الْمَخْطُوطَةِ. وَجَدْتُ هَذِهِ الرِّسَالَةَ (الْكَشْفُ وَالْبَيَانُ) فَأَخْرَجَتْنِي مِنَ الضِّيقِ وَقَرَّبَتِ

---

١) سورة آل عمران الآية (١٩١)

٢) سورة الروم الآية (٦،٧)

Therefore, I undertook the task of editing[12] this treatise, praying that Allah would make it beneficial for Muslims throughout the world and sever the strings of Satan's influence over people. The enemy of Allah assails the human being with a damaging malady in the contemporary world that is known as absentmindedness. In this regard, the Prophet Muhammad ﷺ said, "Knowledge is made deficient through forgetfulness and it is squandered by conveying it to those who are not deserving of it."[13]

This small yet highly beneficial treatise encompasses a vast assortment of knowledge that is rarely found in our time, let alone expressed. It combines a myriad of sacred sciences, such as the skillful citation of Quranic verses, sciences of Hadith, principles of jurisprudence, astronomy, and medicine.

I presented the manuscript of this treatise to the professor of Hadith studies in the College of Uṣūl al-Dīn, Dr. Muṣṭafā ʿUthmān Muhammad. In his response, he said to me, "All of the Hadiths it contains are authentic." I then presented it to the professor of jurisprudence in the College of Sharia, Dr. Kamāl al-ʿAnānī, who said, "Every word in this treatise is accurate."

Encouraged by their validation, I took the initiative to meticulously edit this manuscript, ensuring that it sees the light in the best form possible and benefits the maximum number of students from all corners of the globe who come to study at al-Azhar University.

– Khalid Muhammad Mahmoud

---

12 Although we have relied upon Sheikh Khalid Mahmoud's edition of the text, the IGP team has made many corrections and updates.

13 It was narrated by al-Dārimī in his *Sunan*, vol. 1, p. 150, ʿAbd al-Muḥsin edition, al-Madinah al-Munawwarah and Ibn ʿAbd al-Barr in *Jāmiʿ Bayān al- ʿIlm*, vol. 1, p. 130 on the authority of al-Aʿmash.

الطَّرِيقَ، وَالدَّالُ عَلَى الْخَيْرِ كَفَاعِلِهِ. فَقُمْتُ بِتَحْقِيقِ الرِّسَالَةِ رَاجِياً مِنَ اللهِ تَعَالَى أَنْ يَجْعَلَهَا نَافِعَةً لِلْمُسْلِمِينَ، وَيَقْطَعَ بِهَا حَبَائِلَ الشَّيْطَانِ الْمُسَلَّطِ عَلَى الْإِنْسَانِ بِمَرَضِ الْعَصْرِ وَهُوَ النِّسْيَانُ لِقَوْلِ النَّبِيِّ ﷺ «آفَةُ الْعِلْمِ النِّسْيَانُ وَإِضَاعَتُهُ أَنْ يُحَدِّثَ بِهِ غَيْرُ أَهْلِهِ»[٣] وَقَدْ جَمَعَتْ هَذِهِ الرِّسَالَةُ الصَّغِيرَةُ الْحَجْمِ الْكَبِيرَةُ النَّفْعِ فِي أَحْشَائِهَا عُلُوماً كَثِيرَةً قَلَّمَا يُوجَدُ فِي هَذَا الزَّمَانِ مِثْلُهَا فَقَدْ جَمَعَتْ مِنَ الْعُلُومِ خَوَّاصَ الْقُرْآنِ، وَعِلْمَ الْحَدِيثِ، وَعِلْمَ أُصُولِ الْفِقْهِ، وَعِلْمَ الْفَلَكِ، وَعِلْمَ الطِّبِّ. وَلَقَدْ عَرَضْتُ هَذِهِ الرِّسَالَةَ عَلَى أُسْتَاذِ الْحَدِيثِ بِكُلِّيَةِ أُصُولِ الدِّينِ أ.د/ مُصْطَفَى عُثْمَان مُحَمَّد فَقَالَ إِنَّ هَذِهِ الْأَحَادِيثَ كُلَّهَا صَحِيحَةٌ وَعَرَضْتُهَا عَلَى أُسْتَاذِ الْفِقْهِ بِكُلِّيَةِ الشَّرِيعَةِ أ.د/ كَمَال الْعِنَانِي فَقَالَ لِي كُلُّ كَلِمَةٍ فِي هَذِهِ الرِّسَالَةِ صَحِيحَةٌ وَمِنْ هَذَا الْمُنْطَلَقِ كَانَ اِهْتِمَامِي بِهَذِهِ الْمَخْطُوطَةِ فَجَعَلْتُ أُحَقِّقُهَا لِكَيْ تَرَى النُّورَ وَيَطَّلِعَ عَلَيْهَا أَكْبَرُ عَدَدٍ مُمْكِنٍ مِنَ الطُّلَّابِ الْوَافِدِينَ مِنْ مَشَارِقِ الْأَرْضِ وَمَغَارِبِهَا لِلدِّرَاسَةِ بِالْأَزْهَرِ الشَّرِيفِ وَمَنْ أَرَادَ اللهُ لَهُ أَنْ يَسْتَفِيدَ مِنْ هَذِهِ الرِّسَالَةِ.

---

٣) أخرجه الدارمي في سنته ١ / ١٥٠ - ط عبد المحسن - المدينة المنورة وابن عبد البر في جامع بيان العلم ١ / ١٣٠ - عن الأعمش

Author's Preface

In the Name of Allah, the Most Beneficent, the Most Merciful.

All praise is due to Allah, Who created humankind and predisposed them to forgetfulness. He taught Adam the names, yet He stated concerning him, "But he forgot, and We did not find in him determination."[14] Indeed, forgetfulness is considered a manifestation of perfection for His creation. This is because through it, the contingent and forgetful being has given the eternal Preserver His rightful due. May Allah's blessings and peace be upon our Master Muhammad, who surpassed all creation in both nobility and rank. Allah addressed him, saying, "We will make you recite, and you will not forget."[15]

The contingencies that are possible for others also hold true for him ﷺ, such as lapses and forgetfulness. May Allah ﷻ be pleased with all of his Family, Companions, Followers, those who adhere to his teachings and his partisans. May Allah ﷻ be pleased with all of his Family and Companions as long as any memorizer memorizes and any forgetful person forgets. May Allah ﷻ benefit my people through this compilation.

To proceed: our Sheikh, the complete Imam, the pre-eminent figure, the mighty lion, the unique scholar of the age, the pillar of steadfast scholars, the paragon of accomplished eloquence, our master Shaykh ʿAbd al-Ghanī ibn al-Shaykh Ismāʿīl al-Nābulsī al-Ḥanafī – may Allah benefit us through his abundant knowledge – says:

This is a book that I hastily compiled upon my return from the noble Hajj journey while the Egyptian caravan was preparing to depart, without any delay or procrastination. It was composed in response to a question posed to me in the heavily-populated and safeguarded land of Egypt regarding forgetfulness, which sometimes overwhelms or prevails over a person. It came from the grand vizier, the valiant, lion, the one bestowing passage through the tumultuous corridors of the Ottoman empire, and the summit of Islamic governance: the esteemed minister Ali Pasha. May

---

14 *Ṭā Hā*, 115.

15 *al-Aʿlā*, 6.

مُقَدِّمَةُ الْمُؤَلِّفِ

بِسْمِ اللهِ الرَّحْمَنِ الرَّحِيمِ

الْحَمْدُ للهِ الَّذِي خَلَقَ الْإِنْسَانَ وَطَبَعَهُ عَلَى النِّسْيَانِ وَعَلَّمَ آدَمَ الْأَسْمَاءَ وَقَالَ فِي حَقِّهِ ﴿فَنَسِيَ وَلَمْ نَجِدْ لَهُ عَزْمًا﴾ [٤] حَتَّى قِيلَ أَنَّ النِّسْيَانَ مِنْ كَمَالِ خَلْقِهِ لِأَنَّ الْحَادِثَ النَّاسِيَ قَدْ أَعْطَى الْقَدِيمَ الْحَافِظَ حَقَّهُ وَصَلَّى اللهُ عَلَى سَيِّدِنَا مُحَمَّدٍ الَّذِي فَاقَ الْبَرِيَّةَ نَوْعاً وَجِنْساً وَقَدْ أَنْزَلَ اللهُ عَلَيْهِ خِطَاباً لَهُ ﴿سَنُقْرِئُكَ فَلَا تَنسَىٰ﴾ [٥] وَيَجُوزُ فِي حَقِّهِ عَلَيْهِ الصَّلَاةُ وَالسَّلَامُ الْأَتَمَّانِ الْأَكْمَلَانِ مَا يَجُوزُ فِي حَقِّ غَيْرِهِ مِنَ السَّهْوِ وَالنِّسْيَانِ وَرَضِيَ اللهُ تَعَالَى عَنْ جَمِيعِ آلِهِ وَأَصْحَابِهِ وَسَائِرِ أَتْبَاعِهِ بِالْإِحْسَانِ وَأَحْزَابِهِ وَرَضِيَ اللهُ تَعَالَى عَنْ جَمِيعِ آلِهِ وَأَصْحَابِهِ مَا حَفِظَ حَافِظٌ وَنَسِيَ نَاسٍ وَمَتَّعَ اللهُ تَعَالَى بِمَا أَجْمَعُهُ قَوْمِي وَنَاسِي أَمَّا بَعْدُ: فَيَقُولُ شَيْخُنَا الْإِمَامُ الْكَامِلُ الصَّدْرُ الْمُقَدَّمُ الْهُمَامُ فَرِيدُ الْعَصْرِ وَوَحِيدُ الدَّهْرِ عُمْدَةُ الْعُلَمَاءِ الرَّاسِخِينَ وَقُدْوَةُ الْبُلَغَاءِ الْمُحَقِّقِينَ مَوْلَانَا وَسَيِّدُنَا الشَّيْخُ / عَبْدُ الْغَنِيِّ بْنُ الشَّيْخِ إِسْمَاعِيلَ النَّابُلْسِيُّ الْحَنَفِيُّ نَفَعَنَا اللهُ تَعَالَى بِعُلُومِهِ الْمُنِيفَةِ: هَذَا كِتَابٌ صَنَعْتُهُ بِالْعَجَلَةِ عَقِبَ قُدُومِي مِنَ الْحَجِّ الشَّرِيفِ وَالْقَافِلَةُ الْمِصْرِيَّةُ عَلَى جَنَاحِ السَّفَرِ مِنْ غَيْرِ إِمْهَالٍ وَلَا تَسْوِيفٍ جَوَاباً لِسُؤَالٍ وَرَدَ عَلَيَّ فِي مِصْرَ الْمَحْرُوسَةِ ذَاتِ الرُّبُوعِ الْمَأْنُوسَةِ عَنِ النِّسْيَانِ الَّذِي يَعْرِضُ أَوْ يَغْلِبُ فِي بَعْضِ

---

٤) سورة طه الآية (١١٥)

٥) سورة الأعلى الآية (٦)

Allah facilitate to him the retrieval of every good thing that he desires, preserve him from all harm, and combine for him the best of this world and the Hereafter.

Indeed, he – may Allah ﷻ preserve him – posed to me this query during the days when I had the honour of attending his esteemed assembly in fortified Egypt, gleaming with precious radiance. That happened to be during a visitation from the pole of gnostics, the refuge of the accomplished, of Ṣiddīqī ancestral lineage, the possessor of true knowledge, our master, Imam, Sheikh Zayn al-ʿĀbidīn al-Bakrī. May Allah raise the banners of his glory throughout the horizons and perpetuate the Moon of his brilliant countenance in perfect enlightenment.

During that same time period, I was attending to fellow travellers and companions, and seizing the opportunity to visit the righteous among the living and the deceased, of the noble masters. At that moment, I did not have anything related to this matter in the form of a document or a book. That is, until Allah ﷻ blessed me with the ability to return to my land of Damascus in Shām, may it be spared from all afflictions and calamities over the days to pass.

As such, I have resolved now to grant that noble assembly with this Shāmī composition, which is a foundation of increased good, and the awaited assistance, in accordance with my capacity, inspiration, and guidance. Allah is the One Who facilitates correctness, and from Him is every beginning, every form of succour, and guidance as a whole. I have named it *al-Kashf wa al-Bayān fī mā Yataʿallaq bi al-Nisyān* (*Revelation and Clarification of What Concerns Forgetfulness*). I ask Allah ﷻ to ease the completion of this task and to guide us, along with all Muslims, to the best of paths, and to maintain the elevated position and noble status and rank, both in this world and the Hereafter. This is requested, along with all rich provisions, of the one in whose name it was written and with whose high aspiration and noble mark it has been crowned.

May Allah benefit our brothers and sisters among the Muslims and the believers, purify our hearts and theirs from the effects of forgetfulness, and open for both us and them the preservation of knowledge and the realities of the Qur'an – by the nobility of His righteous Prophets and Messengers, from His presence, with the legislated rulings, and by the

الْأَوْقَاتِ عَلَى الْإِنْسَانِ صَدْرٌ مِنْ جَنَابِ الصَّدْرِ الْأَعْظَمِ وَالْهُمَامِ الضِّرْغَامِ الْمُقَدَّمِ ثَمَرَةُ دَوْحَةِ الدَّوْلَةِ الْعُثْمَانِيَّةِ وَزُبْدَةُ لِبَانِ الْإِمَارَةِ الْإِسْلَامِيَّةِ حَضْرَةُ الْوَزِيرِ عَلِي بَاشَا بَلَّغَهُ اللهُ مِنَ الْخَيْرَاتِ مَا شَاءَ وَحَفِظَهُ مِنْ جَمِيعِ الْأَسْوَاءِ وَجَمَعَ لَهُ بَيْنَ خَيْرَيِ الدُّنْيَا وَالْآخِرَةِ فَإِنَّهُ حَفِظَهُ اللهُ تَعَالَى سَأَلَنِي أَيَّامَ كُنْتُ أَتَشَرَّفُ بِمَجْلِسِهِ الْعَالِي فِي مِصْرَ الْمَأْنُوسَةِ ذَاتِ الْقَدْرِ الْغَالِي وَالنُّورِ الْمُتَلَأْلِئِ وَكَانَ ذَلِكَ بِمَحْضَرٍ مِنْ جَنَابِ قُطْبِ الْعَارِفِينَ وَمَلَاذِ الْكَامِلِينَ سُلَالَةِ النَّسَبِ الصِّدِّيقِيِّ صَاحِبُ الْعِلْمِ الْحَقِيقِيِّ الْمَوْلَى الْإِمَامُ وَالْبَحْرُ الْحَبْرُ الْهُمَامُ الشَّيْخُ زَيْنُ الْعَابِدِينَ الْبَكْرِيُّ رَفَعَ اللهُ تَعَالَى رَايَاتِ مَجْدِهِ فِي الْآفَاقِ وَأَدَامَ قَمَرَ طَلْعَتِهِ الْبَهِيَّةِ فِي كَمَالِ الْإِشْرَاقِ وَكُنْتُ إِذْ ذَاكَ فِي اِشْتِغَالٍ بِالرِّفْقَةِ وَالْأَصْحَابِ وَاغْتِنَامِ زِيَارَةِ الصَّالِحِينَ مِنَ الْأَحْيَاءِ وَالْأَمْوَاتِ مِنَ السَّادَةِ الْأَنْجَابِ وَلَمْ يَكُنْ عِنْدِي فِي ذَلِكَ الْحِينِ مَا يَتَعَلَّقُ بِهَذَا الشَّأْنِ مِنْ صَحِيفَةٍ أَوْ كِتَابٍ حَتَّى مَنَّ اللهُ تَعَالَى عَلَيَّ بِالْعَوْدَةِ إِلَى بِلَادِي دِمَشْقِ الشَّامِ حُمِيَتْ مِنْ جَمِيعِ الْبَلَايَا وَالْمَصَايِبِ عَلَى مَدَا الْأَيَّامِ فَعَزَمْتُ الْآنَ عَلَى إِتْحَافِ ذَلِكَ الْمَجْلِسِ السَّامِي بِهَذَا التَّصْنِيفِ الشَّامِيِّ وَالْخَيْرِ النَّامِيِّ وَالْغَيْثِ الْهَامِيِّ بِحَسَبِ فَتْحِي وَإِلْهَامِي وَاللهُ الْمُوَفِّقُ لِلسَّدَادِ وَمِنْهُ الْبِدَايَةُ وَالْعِنَايَةُ وَالرَّشَادُ وَسَمَّيْتُهُ (**الْكَشْفَ وَالْبَيَانَ فِيمَا يَتَعَلَّقُ بِالنِّسْيَانِ**) وَأَسْأَلُ اللهَ تَعَالَى أَنْ يُيَسِّرَ إِتْمَامَ ذَلِكَ وَأَنْ يَسْلُكَ بِنَا وَبِجَمِيعِ الْمُسْلِمِينَ أَحْسَنَ الْمَسَالِكِ وَأَنْ يُدِيمَ رِفْعَةَ الشَّأْنِ وَعِزَّةَ الْمَكَانَةِ وَالْمَكَانِ فِي الدُّنْيَا وَالْآخِرَةِ مَعَ كَمَالِ السِّيرَةِ الْفَاخِرَةِ لِمَنْ صُنِّفَتْ هَذِهِ الرِّسَالَةُ بِإِسْمِهِ وَتُوِّجَتْ بِعُلُوِّ هِمَّتِهِ وَشَرِيفِ رَسْمِهِ وَأَنْ يَنْفَعَ اللهُ بِهَا إِخْوَانَنَا مِنَ

blessings of the righteous Companions, the great Imams, and the remaining models of the righteous folk from the pious saints, possessors of reverence and modesty throughout the ages.

This book is divided into five chapters and a conclusion:

Chapter 1:
On the Meaning of Forgetfulness – Linguistically and Legally – and the Clarification of That.

Chapter 2:
On the Causes of Forgetfulness and the Verification of the Significance of This Affliction, Which Results in Bewilderment and Absentmindedness.

Chapter 3:
A Mention of the Antidotes for Memory from Quranic Verses, Hadiths, and the Sayings of the Righteous Which Result in the Elimination of Forgetfulness and the Eradication of This Disability.

Chapter 4:
On Physical Medications Mentioned by Physicians for the Treatment of Memory and the Removal of Forgetfulness.

Chapter 5:
The Legal Rulings Arising from Forgetfulness.

Conclusion:
A Clarification That Forgetfulness is not a Blemish on Perfect Human Beings, and That it is Possible for the Prophets ﷺ in Matters They Are Not Obligated to Convey or Relay.[16]

---

16 In the original text, the term ورد (*wurid*) was used, which literally means "it was mentioned".

الْمُسْلِمِينَ وَالْمُسْلِمَاتِ وَالْمُؤْمِنِينَ وَالْمُؤْمِنَاتِ وَأَنْ يُطَهِّرَ قُلُوبَنَا وَقُلُوبَهُمْ مِنْ مُقْتَضَى السَّهْوِ وَالنِّسْيَانِ وَيَفْتَحَ عَلَيْنَا وَعَلَيْهِمْ بِحِفْظِ الْعِلْمِ وَحَقَائِقِ الْقُرْآنِ بِجَاهِ أَنْبِيَّائِهِ الْكِرَامِ وَالْمُرْسَلِينَ مِنْ حَضْرَتِهِ بِشَرَائِعِ الْأَحْكَامِ وَبِبَرَكَةِ الصَّحَابَةِ الْأَئِمَّةِ الْعِظَامِ وَبَقِيَّةِ الصَّالِحِينَ مِنَ الْأَوْلِيَاءِ الصِّدِّيقِينَ أُولِي الْمَهَابَةِ وَالْإِحْتِشَامِ عَلَى مَدَى الْأَيَّامِ. وَقَدْ جَعَلْنَا هَذَا الْكِتَابَ عَلَى خَمْسَةِ فُصُولٍ وَخَاتِمَةٍ:

(**الْفَصْلُ الْأَوَّلُ**) فِي مَعْنَى النِّسْيَانِ - لُغَةً -وَشَرْعًا وَبَيَانِ ذَلِكَ.

(**الْفَصْلُ الثَّانِي**) فِي بَيَانِ أَسْبَابِ النِّسْيَانِ وَتَحْقِيقِ مَعْنَى هَذِهِ الْآفَةِ الْمُقْتَضِيَةِ لِلذُّهُولِ وَالْغَفْلَةِ.

(**الْفَصْلُ الثَّالِثُ**) فِي ذِكْرِ أَدْوِيَةِ الْحِفْظِ الْمُقْتَضِيَّةِ لِزَوَالِ النِّسْيَانِ وَانْتِفَاءِ هَذِهِ الْآفَةِ مِنَ الْآيَاتِ وَالْأَحَادِيثِ وَكَلَامِ الصَّالِحِينَ.

(**الْفَصْلُ الرَّابِعُ**) فِيمَا يَتَعَلَّقُ بِأَدْوِيَةِ الْحِفْظِ. وَإِزَالَةِ النِّسْيَانِ مِمَّا ذَكَرَهُ الْأَطِبَّاءُ مِنَ الدَّوَاءِ الْمَحْسُوسِ.

(**الْفَصْلُ الْخَامِسُ**) فِي الْأَحْكَامِ الشَّرْعِيَّةِ الْمُتَرَتِّبَةِ عَلَى النِّسْيَانِ.

(**الْخَاتِمَةُ**) فِي بَيَانِ أَنَّ النِّسْيَانَ لَيْسَ بِنُقْصَانٍ فِي كَمَالِ الْإِنْسَانِ وَأَنَّهُ يَجُوزُ عَلَى الْأَنْبِيَاءِ عَلَيْهِمُ الصَّلَاةُ وَالسَّلَامُ وَقَدْ وَقَعَ مِنْهُمْ فِي غَيْرِ مَا وَجَبَ عَلَيْهِمْ تَبْلِيغُهُ مِنَ الْأَحْكَامِ وَوُرُودِ [٦] الْآيَاتِ فِي ذَلِكَ وَالْأَخْبَارِ.

---

٦) فى الأصل وورد وثبتت والصحيح المثبت وورود.

Chapter 1: On the Meaning of Forgetfulness

The term النِّسْيَان (forgetfulness) has both linguistic and legislative implications, which we will explain. Linguistically, it is the gerund derived from the root verb نَسِيَ (to forget), which indicates the action of forgetting or overlooking something. According to *al-Qāmūs*,[17] نَسِيَهُ (he forgot) is expressed as نَسْيًا(forgetfully) and نِسْيَانًا(forgetfulness), both marked with a *kasrah*, while نَسْوَةً (they forgot it) is an antonym of حِفْظِهِ (his preservation). النِّسْيُ (forgetting) is denoted by a *kasrah* and refers to what has been forgotten, with النَّسِيُّ (the forgetter) being formed on the same pattern of غَنِيٌّ (rich), signifying one who frequently forgets.

In the lexicon *al-Miṣbāḥ al-Munīr*,[18] it is stated that (النِّسْيَ نَسِيتُ) has two possible meanings: the first involves leaving something due to absent-mindedness or carelessness, as opposed to carefully remembering it. However, the second meaning entails deliberate abandonment. This is evident in the verse "And do not forget kindness among yourselves,"[19] where تَنْسَوُا (forget) implies intentional neglect and disregard, which surpasses mere absent-mindedness or oversight. For instance, forgetting a unit of prayer indicates neglect due to absent-mindedness, but on the other hand a man described as forgetful or a heavily intoxicated person signifies profound negligence.

With regard to its legislative meaning, in his commentary on *Sharḥ al-Manār* in the fundamentals of jurisprudence,[20] the renowned scholar Ibn Mālik stated:

> "(The meaning of) forgetfulness is evident. If an individual possesses intelligence, he can distinguish between forgetfulness and the other states. As a result, it requires no further elaboration. Some argue that forgetfulness is an involuntary condition

---

17 *al-Qāmūs al-Muḥīṭ*.

18 Refer to *al-Miṣbāḥ al-Munīr* by Ibn al-Khaṭīb al-Dahshah.

19 *al-Baqarah*, 237.

20 *Uṣūl al-Fiqh* comprises the knowledge of the general evidences of jurisprudence, the method of extracting rulings from it, and the categories of the rulings extracted therefrom. See *Nihāyah al-Uṣūl* by Al-Isnawī (vol. 1, p. 15).

الْفَصْلُ الْأَوَّلُ فِي مَعْنَى النِّسْيَانِ

النِّسْيَانُ لُغَةً - وَشَرْعاً وَبَيَانُ ذَلِكَ: أَمَّا مَعْنَاهُ لُغَةً فَهُوَ مَصْدَرُ قَوْلِكَ نَسِيَ يَنْسَى قَالَ فِي الْقَامُوسِ: نَسِيَهُ نَسْياً وَنِسْيَاناً وَنِسَاوَةً بِكَسْرِهِنَّ وَنَسْوُهُ ضِدُّ حِفْظِهِ وَأَنْسَاهُ إِيَّاهُ وَالنِّسْيُ بِالْكَسْرِ وَيُفْتَحُ مَا نُسِيَ وَالنَّسِيُّ عَلَى وَزْنِ غَنِيٍّ الْكَثِيرُ النِّسْيَانِ.

وَفِي الْمِصْبَاحِ الْمُنِيرِ[٧] قَالَ: نَسِيتُ النِّسْيَ أَنْسَاهُ نِسْيَاناً مُشْتَرَكٌ بَيْنَ مَعْنَيَيْنِ الْأَوَّلُ تَرْكُ الشَّيْءِ عَلَى ذُهُولٍ وَغَفْلَةٍ وَذَلِكَ خِلَافُ الذَّاكِرِ لَهُ وَالثَّانِي التَّرْكُ عَلَى تَعَمُّدٍ وَمِنْهُ قَوْلُهُ تَعَالَى ﴿وَلَا تَنسَوُا الْفَضْلَ بَيْنَكُمْ﴾[٨] أَيْ لَا تَقْصِدُوا التَّرْكَ وَالْإِهْمَالَ وَيَتَعَدَّى بِالْهَمْزَةِ وَالتَّضْعِيفِ وَنَسِيتُ رَكْعَةً أَهْمَلْتُهَا ذُهُولاً وَرَجُلٌ نَسْيَانٌ وَازِنُ سَكْرَانٍ كَثِيرُ الْغَفْلَةِ.

وَأَمَّا مَعْنَاهُ شَرْعاً: فَقَالَ الْعَلَّامَةُ ابْنُ مَلَكٍ فِي (شَرْحِ الْمَنَارِ) فِي أُصُولِ الْفِقْهِ[٩]: النِّسْيَانُ بَدِيهِيٌّ فَإِنْ كَانَ عَاقِلٌ يُفَرِّقُ بَيْنَهُ وَبَيْنَ غَيْرِهِ فَلَا يَحْتَاجُ إِلَى التَّعْرِيفِ وَقِيلَ هُوَ مَعْنًى يَعْتَرِي الْإِنْسَانَ بِدُونِ اخْتِيَارِهِ فَيُوجِبُ الْغَفْلَةَ

---

٧) انظر المصباح المنير. لابن خطيب الدهشة.

٨) سورة البقرة الآية (٢٣٧).

٩) أصول الفقه: هو معرفة دلائل الفقه إجمالاً وكيفية الاستفادة بها وحال المستفيد / انظر نهاية السول للأسنوى (١/١٥).

that befalls a person, which ultimately leads to negligence in preservation. However, this definition does not apply uniformly, as it may not accurately reflect some situations, such as sleep or unconsciousness.

Alternatively, forgetfulness could be deemed as involuntary ignorance[21] with reference to matters concerning which one was previously aware, despite his awareness of many other matters, and which is not caused by any deficiency. His words, 'despite his awareness...' distinguishes it from sleep and unconsciousness. In addition, his words, 'not caused by any deficiency' distinguish it from mental illness."[22]

In *Mirqāt al-Uṣūl*[23], the author of *al-Durar wa al-Ghurar* stated:

"Forgetfulness is the mind's inability to recall a concept that it has grasped when it occurs to someone who generally can recall it. It encompasses both situations where one is capable of recalling it at any time, which is called 'distractedness (*dhuhūl*)', and situations where one cannot recall without memorizing it anew. The latter is what is termed 'forgetfulness (*nisyān*)' in legal circles."[24]

Moreover, in his commentary on *al-Jāmiʿ al-Ṣaghīr* الجامع الصغير, al-Munāwī states after citing his ﷺ words, "Knowledge is made deficient through forgetfulness and it is squandered by conveying it to those who are not deserving of it[25]:

"Forgetfulness is a form of absentmindedness that results in the removal of acquired information from one's cognizance and recognition, such that one would need to acquire it anew through some means, while distractedness (*sahw*) is a type of

---

21 As opposed to voluntary ignorance, which is termed *jahl*.

22 See *Sharḥ al-Manār* of Ibn Mālik, p. 342.

23 The author seems to have mixed up the titles of Mulla Khusro's Mirqāt al-Wuṣūl and its commentary, *Mir'āh al-Uṣūl* by al-Sharkāsī. He is quoting from the latter.

24 See *Mir'āh al-Uṣūl Sharḥ Mirqāt al-Wuṣūl* by al-Sharkāsī, pp. 329-330.

25 The source of this Hadith has been mentioned previously.

عَنِ الْحِفْظِ، لَكِنْ هَذَا التَّعْرِيفُ غَيْرُ مُضْطَّرِدٍ لِصِدْقِهِ عَلَى النَّوْمِ وَالْإِغْمَاءِ وَقِيلَ: هُوَ جَهْلٌ ضَرُورِيٌّ[١٠] بِمَا كَانَ يَعْلَمُهُ مَعَ عِلْمِهِ بِأُمُورٍ كَثِيرَةٍ لَا بِآفَةٍ إِحْتَرَزَ لِقَوْلِهِ مَعَ عِلْمِهِ[١١] عَنِ النَّوْمِ وَالأَغْمَاءِ بِقَوْلِهِ لَا بِآفَةٍ[١٢] عَنِ الْجُنُونِ وَفِي شَرْحِ (شَرْحُ مِرْقَاةِ الوُصُولِ) لِمُؤَلِّفِ الدُّرَرِ وَالْغُرَرِ قَالَ: النِّسْيَانُ هُوَ عَدَمُ مُلَاحَظَةِ لِلصُّورَةِ الحَاصِلَةِ عِنْدَ العَقْلِ عَمَّا مَنْ شَأْنُهُ المُلَاحَظَةُ فِي الجُمْلَةِ. أَعَمَّ مِنْ أَنْ يَكُونَ مِنْ حَيْثُ يَتَمَكَّنُ مُلَاحَظَتِهَا أَيِّ وَقْتٍ شَاءَ—وَيُسَمَّى هَذَا ذُهُولاً، أَوْ يَكُونُ بِحَيْثُ لَا يُتَمَكَّنُ مِنْ مُلَاحَظَتِهَا إِلَّا بَعْدَ تَجَشُّمِ كَسَبٍ جَدِيدٍ—وَهَذا هُوَ النِّسْيَانُ فِي عُرْفِ الْحُكَمَاءِ وَذَكَرَ الْمُنَاوِيُّ فِي شَرْحِهِ عَلَى (الْجَامِعِ الصَّغِيرِ) عِنْدَ قَوْلِهِ ﷺ «آفَةُ الْعِلْمِ النِّسْيَانُ وَإِضَاعَتُهُ هُوَ أَنْ يُحَدَّثَ بِهِ غَيْرُ أَهْلِهِ»[١٣].

قَالَ: وَالنِّسْيَانُ ذُهُولٌ يَنْتَهِي إِلَى زَوَالِ الْمُدْرَكِ مِنَ الْقُوَّةِ الْمُدْرِكَةِ وَالْحَافِظَةِ بِحَيْثُ يَحْتَاجُ فِي حُصُولِهِ إِلَى سَبَبٍ جَدِيدٍ وَالسَّهْوُ ذُهُولٌ عَنِ الْمُدْرَكِ لَا يَنْتَهِي إِلَى زَوَالِهِ مِنْهَا بَلْ يَنْتَبِهُ بِأَدْنَى تَنْبِيه وَالتَّذَكُّرُ اِسْتِعَادَةُ مَا أثبته الْقَلْبُ لَهُ مِمَّا تَنَحَّى عَنْهُ نِسْيَاناً أَوْ غَفْلَةً ثُمَّ ذَكَرَ الْمُنَاوِيُّ بَعْدَ ذَلِكَ قَالَ: وَقَالَ التَّوْرِيشْتِيُّ: تَرْكُ ضَبْطِ مَا اسْتَوْدَعَ إِمَّا لِضَعْفِ قَلْبِهِ أَوْ عَنْ غَفْلَةٍ أَوْ قَصَدَهُ وَقَالَ الْمَاوَرْدِيُّ:

---

١٠) أي غير مكتسب. انظر شرح المنار لابن ملك ص / ٣٤٢.

١١) ثبت في الأصل يعلمه والصواب ما أثبتناه كما في شرح المنار.

١٢) انظر شرح المنار لابن ملك ص / ٣٤٢.

١٣) سبق تخريج الحديث.

absentmindedness that does not result in its removal. Rather, one would be able to remember it through the slightest reminder. And recollection is to recall something that the heart affirms to dispel forgetfulness and absentmindedness."[26]

He later states[27]:

"Al-Tawrīshtī said, '(Forgetfulness) refers to the lack of preservation of what has been reposited. It can either be due to weakness in one's heart, negligence, or intentional.' Al-Māwardī said, 'Forgetfulness is of two types. The first is borne out of one's conceptual prowess being too weak to preserve that with which the mind is unoccupied. The person whose state is like this is seldom taken into consideration and is often in need of books. The only recourse for someone who has been afflicted with such a condition is patience and reduction (of intake), for it is more likely that he will succeed doing the little he is capable of and being patient. The second stems from neglectful laziness and the actions of the heedless. It is imperative for the one who is afflicted with this to counter his laziness with frequent studying and to remedy his inattention through perpetual watchfulness.' ʿAllāmah Ibn Nujaym stated in *al-Ashbāh wa al-Naẓā'ir* in the section on the rulings pertaining to the forgetful person, 'Forgetfulness is the inability to recall something when it is needed. Scholars disagreed over the distinction that exists between inattentiveness (*sahw*) and forgetfulness (*nisyān*). Nevertheless, the relied upon position is that they are synonyms.'"[28]

---

26 Translator's footnote: This passage is actually from the commentary on a Hadith that occurs previous to this one in al-Munāwī's text, which begins with the text آفَةُ الظَّرْفِ الصَّلَف ("The destruction of status is arrogance").

27 Here, the author is citing from al-Munāwī's commentary verbatim on the Hadith mentioned above.

28 al-Ḥamawī said, "In other words, they impart the same understood meaning, but not in reality" (*al-Ashbāh wa al-Naẓā'ir*, vol. 3, p. 289).

النِّسْيَانُ نَوْعَانِ: (أَحَدُهُمَا يَنْشَأُ عَنْ ضَعْفِ الْقُوَّةِ الْمُتَخَيِّلَةِ عَنْ حِفْظِ مَا يَغْفَلُ عَنْهُ الذِّهْنُ وَمِنْ هَذَا حَالَةً قَلَّ عَنِ الْأَضْدَادِ احْتِجَاجُهُ وَكَثُرَ إِلَى الْكُتُبِ احْتِيَاجُهُ وَلَيْسَ لِمَنْ بُلِيَ بِهِ إِلَّا الصَّبْرُ وَالْإِقْلَالُ لِأَنَّهُ عَلَى الْقَلِيلِ أَقْدَرُ وَبِالصَّبْرِ أَحْرَى أَنْ يَنَالَ وَيَظْفَرَ (وَالثَّانِي) يَحْدُثُ عَنْ غفلة التقصير وَأَعْمَالِ التَّوَانِي فَيَنْبَغِي لِمَنْ ابْتُلِيَ بِهِ اِسْتِدْرَاكُ تَقْصِيرِهِ لِكَثْرَةِ الدَّرْسِ وَإِيقَاظُ غَفْلَتِهِ بِإِدَامَةِ النَّظَرِ وَقَالَ الْعَلَّامَةُ ابْنُ نُجَيمٍ فِي الْأَشْبَاهِ وَالنَّظَائِرِ فِي أَحْكَامِ النَّاسِي إِنَّ النِّسْيَانَ هُوَ عَدَمُ تَذَكُّرِ الشَّيْءِ وَقْتَ حَاجَتِهِ إِلَيْهِ وَاخْتَلَفُوا فِي الْفَرْقِ بَيْنَ السَّهَرِ وَالنِّسْيَانِ وَالْمُعْتَمَدُ أَنَّهُمَا مُتَرَادِفَانِ[١٤].

---

١٤) قال الشيخ الحموي: أي متساويان مفهوماً وما سبق النظر / غمز عيون البصائر على الأشباه والنظائر ٣/٢٨٩.

Chapter 2: An Explanation of the Causes of Forgetfulness and a Clarification of the Meaning of This Ailment Which Amounts to Absent-Mindedness and Negligence

Know[29] that forgetfulness is among the defects of the mind. Physicians cite it among the various diseases of the mind and head. The eminent scholar, Abū ʿAlī Ḥasan ibn Sīnā said in his book *al-Qanun*:

> "Faulty memory, which is forgetfulness, occurs in the posterior part of the brain because it is either a deficiency in one of the brain's functions or a failure in all of them. The primary cause is coldness. When it is mixed with dryness, images cannot be impressed in it. When it is affected with moisture, past matters are not recalled, nor can it record current or temporary matters. Most cases of forgetfulness and faulty memory are attributed to coldness with moisture. However, they can also stem from brain tumours, particularly those associated with coldness."

---

29 He stated this at the beginning due to the importance of what came after it. See *al-Sabʿah Kutub al-Mufīdah* by ʿAlī al-Saqqāf, from p. 63.

الْفَصْلُ الثَّانِي فِي بَيَانِ أَسْبَابِ النِّسْيَانِ وَتَحْقِيقُ مَعْنَى هَذِهِ الْآفَةِ الْمُقْتَضِيَةِ لِلذُّهُولِ وَالْغَفْلَةِ

اِعْلَمْ (١٥) أَنَّ النِّسْيَانَ مِنْ آفَاتِ الدِّمَاغِ وَقَدْ ذَكَرَهُ الْأَطِبَّاءُ مِنْ جُمْلَةِ أَمْرَاضِ الدِّمَاغِ وَالرَّأْسِ حَتَّى قَالَ الرَّئِيسُ أَبُو عَلِيٍّ حَسَنُ ابْنُ سِينَا فِي كِتَابِهِ (الْقَانُونُ): فَسَادُ الذِّكْرِ وَهُوَ النِّسْيَانُ إِنَّمَا يَكُونُ فِي مُؤَخِّرِ الدِّمَاغِ لِأَنَّهُ نُقْصَانٌ فِي فِعْلٍ مِنْ أَفَاعِيلِ الدِّمَاغِ أَوْ بُطْلَانٌ فِي جَمِيعِهِ، وَسَبَبُهُ الْأَوَّلُ هُوَ الْبَرْدُ وَأَمَّا مَعَ يُبُوسَةَ فَلَا يَنْطَبِعُ فِيهِ الْمَثَلُ وَأَمَّا مَعَ رُطُوبَةٍ فَلَا يَحْفَظُ الْأُمُورَ الْمَاضِيَةَ وَلَا يَقْدِرُ عَلَى حِفْظِ الْأُمُورِ الْحَالِيَّةِ وَالْمَوْقِتِيَّةِ وَأَكْثَرُ مَا يَعْرِضُ النِّسْيَانُ وَفَسَادُ الذِّكْرِ عَنْ بَرْدٍ وَرُطُوبَةٍ وَقَدْ يَكُونُ مِنْ أَوْرَامِ الدِّمَاغِ وَخُصُوصاً الْبَارِدَةِ اِنْتَهَى.

---

١٥) أتى بها لشدة الاعتناء بما بعدها. انظر / السبع كتب المفيدة لعلوى السقاف ص ٦٣. ط الحلي

Chapter 3: A Mention of the Treatments for Memorization Which Requires the Removal of Forgetfulness and the Elimination of This Illness from Certain Verses of the Qur'an and Prophetic Ḥadīths and Statements of the Righteous Elect, Which the Scholars Have Tried and Tested and Mentioned in Their Books

A Benefit for Treating Forgetfulness with the Qur'an

One of the beneficial methods for treating forgetfulness is as follows, as mentioned by the esteemed scholar and scrupulous ascetic Imam al-Tamīmī ﷺ regarding the beginning of Sūrah Āl ʿImrān[30]:

"He is the One Who has revealed to you the Book, of which some verses are precise – they are the foundation of the Book – while others are elusive. Those with deviant hearts follow the elusive verses seeking doubt through their interpretations – but none grasps their meaning except Allah. As for those well-grounded in knowledge, they say, 'We believe in this – it is all from our Lord.' But none will be mindful except people of reason. [They say:] 'Our Lord! Do not let our hearts deviate after You have guided us. Grant us Your mercy. You are indeed the Giver. Our Lord! You will certainly gather all humanity for the Day – about which there is no doubt. Surely Allah does not break His promise.'"[31]

These verses possess a special quality of enhancing the memory and dispelling confusion. They are to be written[32] on Friday on a new green dish, using (the ink made of) saffron and rose water. They are then dissolved with the water of a flowing river. The solution is then drunk on an empty stomach before sunrise for seven consecutive days, whereby one should refrain from consuming animal products during that period.

---

30 See the verse in bold within the Arabic section.

31 *Āl ʿImrān*, 7-9.

32 This requires awareness of the sciences related to pens, ink, days, and nights, parallel to the remedies according to the Sunnah.

الْفَصْلُ الثَّالِثُ فِي ذِكْرِ أَدْوِيَةِ الْحِفْظِ الْمُقْتَضِيَّةِ لِزَوَالِ النِّسْيَانِ وَانْتِفَاءِ هَذِهِ الْآفَةِ مِنَ الْآيَاتِ الْقُرْآنِيَّةِ وَالْأَحَادِيثِ النَّبَوِيَّةِ وَكَلَامِ الْأَخْيَارِ مِنَ الصَّالِحِينَ جَرَّبَهَا الْعُلَمَاءُ وَذَكَرُوهَا فِي كُتُبِهِمْ

فَائِدَةٌ لِعِلَاجِ النِّسْيَانِ بِالْقُرْآنِ:

فَمِنْهَا مَا ذَكَرَهُ الشَّيْخُ الْإِمَامُ الْوَرِعُ الزَّاهِدُ التَّمِيمِيُّ رَحِمَهُ اللهُ تَعَالَى فِي أَوَّلِ سُورَةِ آلِ عِمْرَانَ(١٦) ﴿**هُوَ الَّذِي أَنزَلَ عَلَيْكَ الْكِتَابَ مِنْهُ آيَاتٌ مُّحْكَمَاتٌ هُنَّ أُمُّ الْكِتَابِ وَأُخَرُ مُتَشَابِهَاتٌ فَأَمَّا الَّذِينَ فِي قُلُوبِهِمْ زَيْغٌ فَيَتَّبِعُونَ مَا تَشَابَهَ مِنْهُ ابْتِغَاءَ الْفِتْنَةِ وَابْتِغَاءَ تَأْوِيلِهِ وَمَا يَعْلَمُ تَأْوِيلَهُ إِلَّا اللَّهُ وَالرَّاسِخُونَ فِي الْعِلْمِ يَقُولُونَ آمَنَّا بِهِ كُلٌّ مِّنْ عِندِ رَبِّنَا وَمَا يَذَّكَّرُ إِلَّا أُولُو الْأَلْبَابِ ۝ رَبَّنَا لَا تُزِغْ قُلُوبَنَا بَعْدَ إِذْ هَدَيْتَنَا وَهَبْ لَنَا مِن لَّدُنكَ رَحْمَةً ۚ إِنَّكَ أَنتَ الْوَهَّابُ ۝ رَبَّنَا إِنَّكَ جَامِعُ النَّاسِ لِيَوْمٍ لَّا رَيْبَ فِيهِ ۚ إِنَّ اللَّهَ لَا يُخْلِفُ الْمِيعَادَ ۝**﴾

فَإِنَّ هَذِهِ الْآيَاتِ خَاصِّيَتُهَا زِيَادَةُ الْحِفْظِ وَزَوَالُ الْبَلَادَةِ وَمَنْ كَتَبَهَا (١٧) فِي إِنَاءٍ أَخْضَرَ جَدِيدٍ يَوْمَ الْجُمُعَةِ بِزَعْفَرَانٍ وَمَاءِ وَرْدٍ وَمَحَاهَا بِمَاءِ نَهْرٍ جَارِي وَشَرِبَهُ عَلَى الرِّيقِ سَبْعَ مَرَّاتٍ مُتَوَالِيَّاتٍ قَبْلَ طُلُوعِ الشَّمْسِ عَلَى سَبْعِ أَيَّامٍ وَلَا يَأْكُلُ فِي

---

١٦) سورة آل عمران آية ٧ - ٩.

١٧) وينبغي أن تكون عالما بالأقلام والمداد وكذا الأيام والليالي قياسا على العلاج بالسنة.

Whoever does this will achieve their desired outcome.

Another beneficial remedy is found in the following verses in Sūrah Hūd[33]:

"*Alif-Lām-Rā'*. A Book whose verses are well-perfected and then fully explained. From the One [Who is] All-Wise, All-Aware. [Tell them, O Prophet:] 'Worship none but Allah. Surely I am a warner and deliverer of good news to you from Him. And seek your Lord's forgiveness and turn to Him in repentance. He will grant you a good provision for an appointed term and graciously reward the doers of good. But if you turn away, then I truly fear for you the torment of a formidable Day. To Allah is your return. And He is Most Capable of everything.'"[34] These verses enhance one's level of erudition, facilitating the retention of wisdom, eloquence, and comprehension of complex matters. Whoever desires this end, he should write them on a fresh taro leaf with musk and rose water. Then, he should clean the leaf with water from the pitcher he uses to water the taro plant. Afterwards, he should drink the solution. Whoever does that in the morning and the evening for four days, his heart will be expanded such that it can receive knowledge. And he will be able to achieve his objectives.

The following words of Allah ﷻ from Sūrah al-Mu'minūn are effective for memory enhancement and absorbing intricate meanings.

﴿وَلَقَدْ خَلَقْنَا الْإِنسَانَ مِن سُلَالَةٍ مِّن طِينٍ ۝ ثُمَّ جَعَلْنَاهُ نُطْفَةً فِي قَرَارٍ
مَّكِينٍ ۝ ثُمَّ خَلَقْنَا النُّطْفَةَ عَلَقَةً فَخَلَقْنَا الْعَلَقَةَ مُضْغَةً فَخَلَقْنَا الْمُضْغَةَ عِظَامًا
فَكَسَوْنَا الْعِظَامَ لَحْمًا ثُمَّ أَنشَأْنَاهُ خَلْقًا آخَرَ ۚ فَتَبَارَكَ اللَّهُ أَحْسَنُ الْخَالِقِينَ ۝﴾

"And indeed, We created humankind from an extract of clay, then placed each [human] as a sperm-drop in a secure place, then We developed the drop into a clinging clot, then developed the clot into a lump, then developed the lump into bones, then clothed the bones with flesh,

33 See the verse in bold within the Arabic section.

34 *Hūd*, 1-4.

ذَلِكَ النَّهَارِ شَيْئاً فِيهِ رُوحٌ فَكُلُّ مَنْ فَعَلَ ذَلِكَ بَلَغَ مَا أَرَادَ وَمِنْهُ قَوْلُهُ تَعَالَى [١٨] أَوَّلَ سُورَةِ هُودٍ ﴿**الٓر كِتَابٌ أُحْكِمَتْ آيَاتُهُ ثُمَّ فُصِّلَتْ مِن لَّدُنْ حَكِيمٍ خَبِيرٍ ۝ أَلَّا تَعْبُدُوا إِلَّا اللَّهَ إِنَّنِي لَكُم مِّنْهُ نَذِيرٌ وَبَشِيرٌ ۝ وَأَنِ اسْتَغْفِرُوا رَبَّكُمْ ثُمَّ تُوبُوا إِلَيْهِ يُمَتِّعْكُم مَّتَاعًا حَسَنًا إِلَىٰ أَجَلٍ مُّسَمًّى وَيُؤْتِ كُلَّ ذِي فَضْلٍ فَضْلَهُ وَإِن تَوَلَّوْا فَإِنِّي أَخَافُ عَلَيْكُمْ عَذَابَ يَوْمٍ كَبِيرٍ ۝ إِلَى اللَّهِ مَرْجِعُكُمْ وَهُوَ عَلَىٰ كُلِّ شَيْءٍ قَدِيرٌ ۝**﴾ [١٩] هَذِهِ الْآيَاتُ لِتَعَلُّمِ الْعِلْمِ وَتَسْهِيلِ حِفْظِ الْحِكْمَةِ وَالْبَلَاغَةِ وَالْفَصَاحَةِ وَفَهْمِ الْأَشْيَاءِ الْعَوِيصَةِ فَمَنْ أَرَادَ ذَلِكَ فَلْيَكْتُبْهَا فِي وَرَقِ الْقَلْقَاسِ الْأَخْضَرِ بِمِسْكٍ وَمَاءِ وَرْدٍ ثُمَّ يَمْحُو الْوَرَقَةَ مِنْ مَاءٍ بَيْنَ السَّلْقِيَّةِ الَّتِي يَسْقِي مِنْهَا الْقَلْقَاسُ وَيَشْرَبُهُ فَمَنْ فَعَلَ ذَلِكَ أَرْبَعَةَ أَيَّامٍ فِي كُلِّ يَوْمٍ غُدُوًّا وَعَشِيَّةً فَإِنَّهُ يَنْفَتِحُ قَلْبُهُ لِقَبُولِ الْعِلْمِ وَيَنَالُ مَا يُرِيدُهُ وَمِنْهَا قَوْلُ اللهِ تَعَالَى فِي سُورَةِ الْمُؤْمِنُونَ [٢٠] ﴿وَلَقَدْ خَلَقْنَا الْإِنسَانَ مِن سُلَالَةٍ مِّن طِينٍ ۝ ثُمَّ جَعَلْنَاهُ نُطْفَةً فِي قَرَارٍ مَّكِينٍ ۝ ثُمَّ خَلَقْنَا النُّطْفَةَ عَلَقَةً فَخَلَقْنَا الْعَلَقَةَ مُضْغَةً فَخَلَقْنَا الْمُضْغَةَ عِظَامًا فَكَسَوْنَا الْعِظَامَ لَحْمًا ثُمَّ أَنشَأْنَاهُ خَلْقًا آخَرَ ۚ فَتَبَارَكَ اللَّهُ أَحْسَنُ الْخَالِقِينَ ۝﴾ فَإِنَّ هَذِهِ الْآيَاتِ لِلْحِفْظِ وَفَهْمِ الْمَعَانِي الدَّقِيقَةِ فَمَنْ أَرَادَ الْعَمَلَ بِذَلِكَ فَلْيَكْتُبْ هَذِهِ الْآيَاتِ فِي إِنَاءٍ وَيَصُمْ سَبْعَةَ أَيَّامٍ لَا يَأْكُلُ عِنْدَ فِطْرِهِ شَيْئاً فِيهِ رُوحٌ وَيُفْطِرُ عَلَى مَا مُحِيَ بِهِ ذَلِكَ الْإِنَاءُ الْمَكْتُوبُ ثُمَّ يَأْخُذُ الْكُنْدُرَ الذَّكَرَ وَمِنْ

١٨) سورة هود الآية رقم (١) إلى الآية رقم (٤)

١٩) انظر الدر النظيم ومنافع القرآن العظيم للتميمي مخطوطة تحت رقم ٣١٦٢ دار الكتب.

٢٠) سورة المؤمنون الآية رقم (١٢) إلى الآية رقم (١٤)

then We brought it into being as a new creation. So Blessed is Allah, the Best of Creators."[35] Whoever desires to act upon that, then let him write these verses on a vessel, and then fast for seven days, not consuming anything therein of animal origin at the time of breaking the fast. He should then break his fast with what has been wiped out from the vessel. Then he should take a part equal to ten seeds of wild frankincense, a part equal to twenty dirhams of the heart of the pistachio, and four *mithqāls* of sugar, and grind them all to a fine powder. Then they are to be placed in a pot made of clay, with apple water then being poured over them; the ingredients should be boiled until they become a syrup. The syrup should then be lifted and placed in a green pottery jar. And in the last third of every night, he is to boil an ounce of it with sweet fennel and cumin and drink it, for it is very beneficial. It is even moreso beneficial than the seed of watercress, by the permission of Allah Almighty and the blessing of the Noble Qur'an.

Another method is to use the following verses of Sūrah al-Qaṣaṣ[36]:

"Indeed, We have steadily delivered the Word to the people so they may be mindful. Those to whom We had given the Scripture before this, they do believe in it. When it is recited to them, they declare, 'We believe in it. This is definitely the truth from our Lord. We had already submitted before this.' These will be given a double reward for their perseverance, responding to evil with good, and for donating from what We have provided for them. When they hear slanderous talk, they turn away from it, saying, 'We are accountable for our deeds and you for yours. Peace to you! We want nothing to do with those who act ignorantly.'"[37] The special benefit imparted from these verses is the endowment of wisdom, memorization, and the understanding of subtle meanings. Whoever wishes to use them for that purpose should fast for three days, beginning on the first Thursday of the month. He should then proceed to write these verses in a glass container and wipe them out with water from a flowing river.

35 *al-Mu'minūn*, 12-14.

36 See the verse in bold within the Arabic section.

37 *al-Qaṣaṣ*, 51-55.

حَبِّ الطِّينِ الطَّيِّبِ جُزْءً قَدْرَ عَشْرَ حَبَّاتٍ وَمِنْ قَلْبِ الْفُسْتُقِ الطَّرِيِّ عِشْرُونَ دِرْهَماً وَمِنْ عِرْقِ السُّوسِ أَرْبَعَ مَثَاقِيلَ مِنَ السُّكَّرِ الطَّبَرْزِ وَثَلَاثِينَ مِثْقَالاً وَيَدُقُّ الْجَمِيعَ دَقّاً نَاعِماً وَيُوضَعُ فِي قِدْرٍ مِنْ حَجَرٍ فَخَارٍ وَيُلْقِي عَلَيْهِ مَاءَ التُّفَّاحِ وَيَطْبُخُهُ شَرَاباً إِلَى أَنْ يَسْتَحْكِمَ ثُمَّ يُرْفَعُ فِي بُرْنِيَّةٍ خَضْرَاءَ [٢١] وَيَسْتَعْمِلُ مِنْهُ كُلَّ لَيْلَةٍ عِنْدَ السَّحَرِ وَهُوَ الثُّلُثُ الْأَخِيرُ مِنَ اللَّيْلِ قَدْرَ أُوقِيَّةٍ وَيَشْرَبُ عَلَيْهِ مَا قَدْ غَلَى فِيهِ الْحَبَّةَ الْحُلْوَةَ وَالشَّمَّارَ فَإِنَّهُ نَافِعٌ جِدّاً أَنْفَعَ مِنْ حَبِّ الْبَلَادِرِ بِإِذْنِ اللهِ تَعَالَى وَبِبَرَكَةِ الْقُرْآنِ الْكَرِيمِ وَمِنْهَا قَوْلُهُ تَعَالَى فِي سُورَةِ الْقَصَصِ [٢٢] ﴿**وَلَقَدْ وَصَّلْنَا لَهُمُ الْقَوْلَ لَعَلَّهُمْ يَتَذَكَّرُونَ ۝ الَّذِينَ آتَيْنَاهُمُ الْكِتَابَ مِن قَبْلِهِ هُم بِهِ يُؤْمِنُونَ ۝ وَإِذَا يُتْلَىٰ عَلَيْهِمْ قَالُوا آمَنَّا بِهِ إِنَّهُ الْحَقُّ مِن رَّبِّنَا إِنَّا كُنَّا مِن قَبْلِهِ مُسْلِمِينَ ۝ أُولَٰئِكَ يُؤْتَوْنَ أَجْرَهُم مَّرَّتَيْنِ بِمَا صَبَرُوا وَيَدْرَءُونَ بِالْحَسَنَةِ السَّيِّئَةَ وَمِمَّا رَزَقْنَاهُمْ يُنفِقُونَ ۝ وَإِذَا سَمِعُوا اللَّغْوَ أَعْرَضُوا عَنْهُ وَقَالُوا لَنَا أَعْمَالُنَا وَلَكُمْ أَعْمَالُكُمْ سَلَامٌ عَلَيْكُمْ لَا نَبْتَغِي الْجَاهِلِينَ ۝**﴾ فَإِنَّ خَاصِيَّةَ هَذِهِ الْآيَاتِ الْحِكْمَةُ وَحِفْظُ الْمَعَانِي الدَّقِيقَةِ وَفَهْمُهَا وَمَنْ أَرَادَ الْعَمَلَ بِذَلِكَ فَلْيَصُمْ ثَلَاثَةَ أَيَّامٍ أَوَّلُهَا الْخَمِيسُ مِنْ أَوَّلِ الشَّهْرِ وَلْيَكْتُبْ هَذِهِ الْآيَاتِ فِي إِنَاءِ زُجَاجٍ وَيَمْحُوهُ بِمَاءِ نَهْرٍ جَارِي وَيَشْرَبُهُ كُلَّ لَيْلَةٍ قَبْلَ طُلُوعِ الْفَجْرِ فَإِنَّهُ يُؤَثِّرُ تَأْثِيرًا حَسَنًا مُبَارَكًا وَمِنْهَا قَوْلُهُ تَعَالَى فِي سُورَةِ الشُّورَى [٢٣] ﴿وَكَذَٰلِكَ أَوْحَيْنَا إِلَيْكَ

---

٢١) إناء من الفخار الأخضر اللون.

٢٢) سورة القصص الآية رقم (٥١) إلى الآية رقم (٥٥).

٢٣) سورة الشورى الآية رقم (٥٢) إلى الآية (٥٣)

Thereafter, he should drink it every night before dawn. It will ultimately have an excellent, blessed effect.

Another method is using the following words of Allah found in Sūrah al-Shūrā:

﴿وَكَذَٰلِكَ أَوْحَيْنَا إِلَيْكَ رُوحًا مِّنْ أَمْرِنَا مَا كُنتَ تَدْرِي مَا الْكِتَابُ وَلَا الْإِيمَانُ وَلَٰكِن جَعَلْنَاهُ نُورًا نَّهْدِي بِهِ مَن نَّشَاءُ مِنْ عِبَادِنَا وَإِنَّكَ لَتَهْدِي إِلَىٰ صِرَاطٍ مُّسْتَقِيمٍ ۝ صِرَاطِ اللَّهِ الَّذِي لَهُ مَا فِي السَّمَاوَاتِ وَمَا فِي الْأَرْضِ أَلَا إِلَى اللَّهِ تَصِيرُ الْأُمُورُ ۝﴾

"And so We have sent to you a revelation by Our command. You did not know of [this] Book and faith. But We have made it a light, by which We guide whoever We will of Our servants. And you are truly leading to the Straight Path – the Path of Allah, to Whom belongs whatever is in the Heavens and whatever is on the earth. Surely to Allah all matters will return."[38] These verses are especially useful for memorizing what one has forgotten, whereby one will be able to gain knowledge after ignorance and alertness after negligence. Whoever desires this end should write these verses in a glass container with saffron and rose water. Then, bee's honey is added and it is all erased with water. Thereafter, he should drink the mixture for three consecutive Fridays after the dawn prayer. Each Friday, he is advised to drink three gulps of it. That will be effective, by the blessing of the Noble Qur'an.

Another method is the following series of verses of Sūrah al-Najm[39]. Sūrah al-Najm has specific qualities that aid in wisdom retention, understanding intricate meanings, and awakening from heedlessness. Here is a method for harnessing their benefits.

"By the stars when they fade away! Your fellow man is neither misguided nor astray. Nor does he speak of his own whims. It is only a

38 *al-Shūrā*, 52-53.

39 See the verse in bold within the Arabic section.

رُوحًا مِّنْ أَمْرِنَا مَا كُنتَ تَدْرِي مَا الْكِتَابُ وَلَا الْإِيمَانُ وَلَٰكِن جَعَلْنَاهُ نُورًا نَّهْدِي بِهِ مَن نَّشَاءُ مِنْ عِبَادِنَا وَإِنَّكَ لَتَهْدِي إِلَىٰ صِرَاطٍ مُّسْتَقِيمٍ ۝ صِرَاطِ اللَّهِ الَّذِي لَهُ مَا فِي السَّمَاوَاتِ وَمَا فِي الْأَرْضِ أَلَا إِلَى اللَّهِ تَصِيرُ الْأُمُورُ ۝﴾ فَإِنَّ خَاصِيَّةَ هَذِهِ الْآيَةِ لِلْحِفْظِ بَعْدَ النِّسْيَانِ وَالْعِلْمِ بَعْدَ الْجَهْلِ وَالتَّنْبِيهِ بَعْدَ الْغَفْلَةِ فَمَنْ أَرَادَ ذَلِكَ فَلْيَكْتُبْهَا فِي إِنَاءِ زُجَاجٍ بِزَعْفَرَانٍ وَمَاءِ وَرْدٍ وَيَضَعُ فِيهِ عَسَلَ النَّحْلِ ثُمَّ يَمْحُوهُ وَيَشْرَبُهُ يَفْعَلُ ذَلِكَ ثَلَاثَ جُمَعٍ بَعْدَ صَلَاةِ الصُّبْحِ كُلَّ جُمُعَةٍ ثَلَاثَ جُرَعٍ فَإِنَّهُ يُؤَثِّرُ بِبَرَكَةِ الْقُرْآنِ الْكَرِيمِ وَمِنْهَا قَوْلُهُ تَعَالَى [٢٤] ﴿وَالنَّجْمِ إِذَا هَوَىٰ ۝ مَا ضَلَّ صَاحِبُكُمْ وَمَا غَوَىٰ ۝ وَمَا يَنطِقُ عَنِ الْهَوَىٰ ۝ إِنْ هُوَ إِلَّا وَحْيٌ يُوحَىٰ ۝ عَلَّمَهُ شَدِيدُ الْقُوَىٰ ۝ ذُو مِرَّةٍ فَاسْتَوَىٰ ۝ وَهُوَ بِالْأُفُقِ الْأَعْلَىٰ ۝ ثُمَّ دَنَا فَتَدَلَّىٰ ۝ فَكَانَ قَابَ قَوْسَيْنِ أَوْ أَدْنَىٰ ۝ فَأَوْحَىٰ إِلَىٰ عَبْدِهِ مَا أَوْحَىٰ ۝ مَا كَذَبَ الْفُؤَادُ مَا رَأَىٰ ۝ أَفَتُمَارُونَهُ عَلَىٰ مَا يَرَىٰ ۝ وَلَقَدْ رَآهُ نَزْلَةً أُخْرَىٰ ۝ عِندَ سِدْرَةِ الْمُنتَهَىٰ ۝ عِندَهَا جَنَّةُ الْمَأْوَىٰ ۝ إِذْ يَغْشَى السِّدْرَةَ مَا يَغْشَىٰ ۝ مَا زَاغَ الْبَصَرُ وَمَا طَغَىٰ ۝ لَقَدْ رَأَىٰ مِنْ آيَاتِ رَبِّهِ الْكُبْرَىٰ ۝﴾ فَإِنَّ خَاصِيَّةَ هَذِهِ الْآيَاتِ أَنَّهَا تُقَوِّي الذِّهْنَ وَتُصَفِّي الْقَلْبَ وَتُزِيلُ النِّسْيَانَ فَمَنْ أَرَادَ الْعَمَلَ بِذَلِكَ فَلْيَكْتُبْ ذَلِكَ فِي إِنَاءِ زُجَاجٍ بِمِسْكٍ وَمَاءِ وَرْدٍ وَيَمْحُوهُ بِمَاءِ زَمْزَمَ أَوْ مَاءِ عَيْنِ سَلْوَانَ وَيَشْرَبُ مِنْهُ سَبْعَةَ أَيَّامٍ مُتَوَالِيَاتٍ بَعْدَ صَلَاةِ الْفَجْرِ وَيَكُونُ عَلَى الرِّيقِ فَإِنَّهُ

---

٢٤) سورة النجم الآية رقم (١) إلى الآية رقم (١٨).

revelation sent down. He has been taught by one of mighty power and great perfection, who once rose to true form while on the highest point above the horizon, then he approached [the Prophet], coming so close that he was only two arms-lengths away or even less. Then Allah revealed to His servant what He revealed. The [Prophet's] heart did not doubt what he saw. How can you then dispute with him regarding what he saw? And he certainly saw that a second time at the Lote Tree of the most extreme limit [in the seventh heaven] – near which is the Garden of Residence – while the Lote Tree was overwhelmed with splendours! The [Prophet's] sight never wandered, nor did it overreach. He certainly saw some of his Lord's greatest signs."[40] The special qualities of these verses is found in the fact that they strengthen the mind, purify the heart, and remove forgetfulness. Whoever wishes to act upon that, should write these verses in a glass container with musk, rose water, and then dissolve them in Zamzam water or water from the spring of Salwān. He should drink from this mixture for seven consecutive days after the Fajr prayer, drinking it on an empty stomach. By following this prescription, one can achieve their desired goal.

There are also the verses from Sūrah al-Raḥmān verses 1 to 76[41]. These verses are most effective for enhancing one's memorization and intelligence. Whoever desires to use them for this objective should take some squeezed black grapes, in whatever quantity he desires. He should then mix it with an amount of sugar equivalent to half of it, and a volume of honey up to half of that and a quantity of apple juice equivalent to a quarter of that. All of the aforementioned ingredients are to be combined; and for every *raṭl*,[42] a weight equivalent to a dirham of saffron, a dirham of cinnamon, a dirham of anise, a dirham of rose, a dirham of pepper, and a quarter dirham of stone musk should be added. The entire mixture is then blended, placed in a pot, and boiled until only half of it remains. The verses are then engraved in a glass jar with saffron, musk, and rose water,

---

40 *al-Najm*, 1-18.

41 See the verses in bold within the Arabic section.

42 Translator's note: A *raṭl* is a measure of weight equivalent to around 453 grams.

يَبْلُغ مُرَادَهُ. وَمِنْهَا قَوْلُهُ تَعَالَى[٢٥]

﴿الرَّحْمَٰنُ ۝ عَلَّمَ الْقُرْآنَ ۝ خَلَقَ الْإِنسَانَ ۝ عَلَّمَهُ الْبَيَانَ ۝ الشَّمْسُ وَالْقَمَرُ بِحُسْبَانٍ ۝ وَالنَّجْمُ وَالشَّجَرُ يَسْجُدَانِ ۝ وَالسَّمَاءَ رَفَعَهَا وَوَضَعَ الْمِيزَانَ ۝ أَلَّا تَطْغَوْا فِي الْمِيزَانِ ۝ وَأَقِيمُوا الْوَزْنَ بِالْقِسْطِ وَلَا تُخْسِرُوا الْمِيزَانَ ۝ وَالْأَرْضَ وَضَعَهَا لِلْأَنَامِ ۝ فِيهَا فَاكِهَةٌ وَالنَّخْلُ ذَاتُ الْأَكْمَامِ ۝ وَالْحَبُّ ذُو الْعَصْفِ وَالرَّيْحَانُ ۝ فَبِأَيِّ آلَاءِ رَبِّكُمَا تُكَذِّبَانِ ۝ خَلَقَ الْإِنسَانَ مِن صَلْصَالٍ كَالْفَخَّارِ ۝ وَخَلَقَ الْجَانَّ مِن مَّارِجٍ مِّن نَّارٍ ۝ فَبِأَيِّ آلَاءِ رَبِّكُمَا تُكَذِّبَانِ ۝ رَبُّ الْمَشْرِقَيْنِ وَرَبُّ الْمَغْرِبَيْنِ ۝ فَبِأَيِّ آلَاءِ رَبِّكُمَا تُكَذِّبَانِ ۝ مَرَجَ الْبَحْرَيْنِ يَلْتَقِيَانِ ۝ بَيْنَهُمَا بَرْزَخٌ لَّا يَبْغِيَانِ ۝ فَبِأَيِّ آلَاءِ رَبِّكُمَا تُكَذِّبَانِ ۝ يَخْرُجُ مِنْهُمَا اللُّؤْلُؤُ وَالْمَرْجَانُ ۝ فَبِأَيِّ آلَاءِ رَبِّكُمَا تُكَذِّبَانِ ۝ وَلَهُ الْجَوَارِ الْمُنشَآتُ فِي الْبَحْرِ كَالْأَعْلَامِ ۝ فَبِأَيِّ آلَاءِ رَبِّكُمَا تُكَذِّبَانِ ۝ كُلُّ مَنْ عَلَيْهَا فَانٍ ۝ وَيَبْقَىٰ وَجْهُ رَبِّكَ ذُو الْجَلَالِ وَالْإِكْرَامِ ۝ فَبِأَيِّ آلَاءِ رَبِّكُمَا تُكَذِّبَانِ ۝ يَسْأَلُهُ مَن فِي السَّمَاوَاتِ وَالْأَرْضِ ۚ كُلَّ يَوْمٍ هُوَ فِي شَأْنٍ ۝ فَبِأَيِّ آلَاءِ رَبِّكُمَا تُكَذِّبَانِ ۝ سَنَفْرُغُ لَكُمْ أَيُّهَ الثَّقَلَانِ ۝ فَبِأَيِّ آلَاءِ رَبِّكُمَا تُكَذِّبَانِ ۝ يَا مَعْشَرَ الْجِنِّ وَالْإِنسِ إِنِ اسْتَطَعْتُمْ أَن تَنفُذُوا مِنْ أَقْطَارِ السَّمَاوَاتِ وَالْأَرْضِ فَانفُذُوا ۚ لَا تَنفُذُونَ إِلَّا بِسُلْطَانٍ ۝ فَبِأَيِّ آلَاءِ رَبِّكُمَا تُكَذِّبَانِ ۝ يُرْسَلُ عَلَيْكُمَا شُوَاظٌ مِّن نَّارٍ وَنُحَاسٌ فَلَا تَنتَصِرَانِ ۝ فَبِأَيِّ آلَاءِ رَبِّكُمَا تُكَذِّبَانِ ۝ فَإِذَا انشَقَّتِ السَّمَاءُ فَكَانَتْ وَرْدَةً كَالدِّهَانِ ۝ فَبِأَيِّ آلَاءِ رَبِّكُمَا تُكَذِّبَانِ ۝ فَيَوْمَئِذٍ لَّا يُسْأَلُ عَن ذَنبِهِ إِنسٌ وَلَا جَانٌّ ۝ فَبِأَيِّ آلَاءِ رَبِّكُمَا تُكَذِّبَانِ ۝ يُعْرَفُ الْمُجْرِمُونَ بِسِيمَاهُمْ فَيُؤْخَذُ بِالنَّوَاصِي وَالْأَقْدَامِ ۝ فَبِأَيِّ آلَاءِ رَبِّكُمَا تُكَذِّبَانِ ۝ هَٰذِهِ جَهَنَّمُ الَّتِي يُكَذِّبُ بِهَا الْمُجْرِمُونَ ۝ يَطُوفُونَ بَيْنَهَا وَبَيْنَ حَمِيمٍ آنٍ ۝ فَبِأَيِّ آلَاءِ رَبِّكُمَا تُكَذِّبَانِ ۝ وَلِمَنْ خَافَ مَقَامَ رَبِّهِ جَنَّتَانِ ۝ فَبِأَيِّ آلَاءِ رَبِّكُمَا تُكَذِّبَانِ ۝ ذَوَاتَا أَفْنَانٍ ۝ فَبِأَيِّ آلَاءِ رَبِّكُمَا تُكَذِّبَانِ ۝ فِيهِمَا عَيْنَانِ تَجْرِيَانِ ۝ فَبِأَيِّ آلَاءِ رَبِّكُمَا تُكَذِّبَانِ ۝ فِيهِمَا مِن كُلِّ فَاكِهَةٍ زَوْجَانِ ۝ فَبِأَيِّ آلَاءِ رَبِّكُمَا تُكَذِّبَانِ ۝ مُتَّكِئِينَ عَلَىٰ فُرُشٍ بَطَائِنُهَا مِنْ إِسْتَبْرَقٍ ۚ وَجَنَى الْجَنَّتَيْنِ دَانٍ ۝ فَبِأَيِّ آلَاءِ رَبِّكُمَا تُكَذِّبَانِ ۝ فِيهِنَّ قَاصِرَاتُ الطَّرْفِ لَمْ يَطْمِثْهُنَّ إِنسٌ قَبْلَهُمْ وَلَا جَانٌّ ۝ فَبِأَيِّ آلَاءِ رَبِّكُمَا تُكَذِّبَانِ ۝ كَأَنَّهُنَّ الْيَاقُوتُ وَالْمَرْجَانُ ۝ فَبِأَيِّ آلَاءِ رَبِّكُمَا تُكَذِّبَانِ ۝ هَلْ جَزَاءُ الْإِحْسَانِ إِلَّا الْإِحْسَانُ ۝ فَبِأَيِّ

---

٢٥) سورة الرحمن الآية رقم (١) إلى الآية رقم (٧٦).

after which the writing is dissolved with rose water. This is added to the aforementioned essence and used before sleep. It will be an aid for him to achieve his objective and he will attain a solid understanding of whatever he wishes.

Another formula is found in the following verses of Sūrah al-Fajr:

﴿وَالْفَجْرِ ۝ وَلَيَالٍ عَشْرٍ ۝ وَالشَّفْعِ وَالْوَتْرِ ۝ وَاللَّيْلِ إِذَا يَسْرِ ۝ هَلْ فِي ذَٰلِكَ قَسَمٌ لِّذِي حِجْرٍ ۝﴾

"By the dawn, and the ten nights, and the even and the odd, and the night when it passes! Is all this a sufficient oath for those who have sense?"[43] These verses are an effective aid for both memorization and the prevention of forgetfulness. Those intending to benefit from them should write them on a glass vessel filled with the fresh juice of ās[44] grapes and saffron. Subsequently, they should be washed with bee's honey along with fresh and ripe grape juice. He should then drink from this solution, for it will purify his mind and increase his understanding.

***

43 *al-Fajr*, 1-5.

44 *al-Ās*: A type of grapes.

آلَاءِ رَبِّكُمَا تُكَذِّبَانِ ۝ وَمِن دُونِهِمَا جَنَّتَانِ ۝ فَبِأَيِّ آلَاءِ رَبِّكُمَا تُكَذِّبَانِ ۝ مُدْهَامَّتَانِ ۝ فَبِأَيِّ آلَاءِ رَبِّكُمَا تُكَذِّبَانِ ۝ فِيهِمَا عَيْنَانِ نَضَّاخَتَانِ ۝ فَبِأَيِّ آلَاءِ رَبِّكُمَا تُكَذِّبَانِ ۝ فِيهِمَا فَاكِهَةٌ وَنَخْلٌ وَرُمَّانٌ ۝ فَبِأَيِّ آلَاءِ رَبِّكُمَا تُكَذِّبَانِ ۝ فِيهِنَّ خَيْرَاتٌ حِسَانٌ ۝ فَبِأَيِّ آلَاءِ رَبِّكُمَا تُكَذِّبَانِ ۝ حُورٌ مَّقْصُورَاتٌ فِي الْخِيَامِ ۝ فَبِأَيِّ آلَاءِ رَبِّكُمَا تُكَذِّبَانِ ۝ لَمْ يَطْمِثْهُنَّ إِنسٌ قَبْلَهُمْ وَلَا جَانٌّ ۝ فَبِأَيِّ آلَاءِ رَبِّكُمَا تُكَذِّبَانِ ۝ مُتَّكِئِينَ عَلَىٰ رَفْرَفٍ خُضْرٍ وَعَبْقَرِيٍّ حِسَانٍ ۝﴾.

فَإِنَّ خَاصِيَّةَ هَذِهِ الْآيَاتِ لِلْحِفْظِ وَالذَّكَاءِ فَمَنْ أَرَادَ الْعَمَلَ بِذَلِكَ فَلْيَأْخُذْ مِنْ عَصِيرِ الْعِنَبِ الْأَسْوَدِ مَا يُرِيدُ وَيَأْخُذُ مِثْلَ نِصْفِهِ سُكَّراً وَمِثْلَ نِصْفِهِ عَسَلَ نَحْلٍ وَمِثْلَ رُبْعِهِ مَاءَ سَفَرْجَلٍ وَمِثْلَ رُبْعِهِ مَاءَ تُفَّاحٍ ثُمَّ يَجْمَعُ الْجَمِيعَ وَيَأْخُذُ لِكُلِّ رَطْلٍ وَزْنَ دِرْهَمٍ زَعْفَرَانٍ (شَعْرٌ) وَدِرْهَمَ دَارِ صِينِيٍّ وَدِرْهَمَ أَنِيسُونٍ وَدِرْهَمَ وَرْدٍ وَدِرْهَمَ فُلْفُلٍ وَرُبْعَ دِرْهَمٍ مِسْكٍ حَجَرٍ ثُمَّ يَخْلِطُ الْجَمِيعَ وَيُوضَعُ فِي قِدْرٍ وَيُغْلَى عَلَيْهِ حَتَّى يَبْقَى نِصْفُهُ ثُمَّ يَكْتُبُ الْآيَاتِ فِي جَامِ زُجَاجٍ بِزَعْفَرَانٍ وَمِسْكٍ وَمَاءِ وَرْدٍ ثُمَّ يَمْحِي الْكِتَابَةَ بِمَاءِ وَرْدٍ يُضَافُ ذَلِكَ إِلَى الْعَصِيرِ الْمَذْكُورِ وَيَسْتَعْمِلُ مِنْهُ عِنْدَ النَّوْمِ فَإِنَّهُ يَبْلُغُ الْغَرَضَ وَيَحْصُلُ لَهُ الْفَهْمُ الْكَثِيرُ فِيمَا يُرِيدُهُ. وَمِنْهَا قَوْلُهُ تَعَالَى [٢٦] ﴿وَالْفَجْرِ وَلَيَالٍ عَشْرٍ وَالشَّفْعِ وَالْوَتْرِ وَاللَّيْلِ إِذَا يَسْرِي هَلْ فِي ذَلِكَ قَسَمٌ لِذِي حِجْرٍ﴾ فَإِنَّ هَذِهِ الْآيَاتِ لِلْحِفْظِ وَزَوَالِ النِّسْيَانِ، فَمَنْ أَرَادَ الْعَمَلَ بِذَلِكَ فَلْيَكْتُبْهَا فِي إِنَاءِ زُجَاجٍ بِمَاءِ آسٍ وَزَعْفَرَانٍ وَيَمْحُوهُ بِعَسَلِ النَّحْلِ وَعَصِيرِ عِنَبٍ طَرِيٍّ لِوَقْتِهِ وَيَشْرَبُ مِنْهُ فَإِنَّهُ يَصْفُو ذِهْنُهُ وَيَكْثُرُ فَهْمُهُ.

* * *

٢٦) سورة الفجر الآية رقم (١) إلى رقم (٥).

A Benefit for Treating Forgetfulness Through the Sunnah

It is narrated in a Hadith that the Prophet Muhammad ﷺ said, as reported by al-Tirmidhī in his *Sunan* from Aḥmad ibn al-Ḥasan, who narrated from Sulaymān ibn ʿAbd al-Raḥmān al-Dimashqī, who narrated from al-Walīd ibn Muslim, who narrated from Jurayj, from ʿAṭā' ibn Abī Rabāḥ, and from ʿIkrimah, the freed slave of Ibn ʿAbbās, who narrated from Ibn ʿAbbās, who said: "While we were with the Messenger of Allah ﷺ, ʿAlī ibn Abī Ṭālib came and said: 'By my father and mother, O Messenger of Allah, something like a veil has been cast over my heart, and I do not find myself capable of grasping the Qur'an as I used to. So, teach me words through which Allah may benefit me, and benefit others through me, and establish firmly what I have learned within my heart.' The Messenger of Allah ﷺ said to him: 'O Abū al-Ḥasan, shall I not teach you some words which Allah may benefit you with, and benefit others through you, and establish firmly what you have learned within your heart?' He said: 'Certainly, O Messenger of Allah, teach me.' He said: 'When the night of Friday approaches, if you can manage to stand during its last third and pray, then do so, for it is an hour when supplications are granted. My brother, Yaʿqūb, advised his sons: "I will seek forgiveness for you from my Lord. Indeed, He is the Forgiving, the Merciful"[45] until the night of Friday comes. If you cannot do so, then stand in the middle of it. If you are unable to do even that, then stand at the beginning of it and pray four *rakʿahs*. In the first *rakʿah*, recite Sūrah Yā Sīn after al-Fātiḥah, in the second *rakʿah*, recite al-Fātiḥah and Hā' Mīm al-Dukhān, in the third *rakʿah*, recite al-Fātiḥah and Sūrah al-Jumuʿah, and in the fourth *rakʿah*, recite al-Fātiḥah and Tabārak. After completing the *tashahhud*, praise Allah, glorify Him, send blessings upon me and upon all the Prophets, seek forgiveness for the believing men and believing women, and for your brothers who preceded you in faith. Then say at the end of that: O Allah, have mercy on me by keeping me away from sins as long as You keep me alive, and have mercy on me by not burdening me with what does not concern me, and grant me the beauty of

---

45 *Yūsuf*, 98.

فَائِدَةٌ لِعِلَاجِ النِّسْيَانِ مِنْ خِلَالِ السُّنَّةِ

وَوَرَدَ فِي الْأَحَادِيثِ عَنْ رَسُولِ اللهِ ﷺ أَشْيَاءُ مِنْ ذَلِكَ فَمِنْهَا مَا أَخْرَجَهُ التِّرْمِذِيُّ فِي سُنَنِهِ عَنْ أَحْمَدَ بْنِ الْحَسَنِ قَالَ حَدَّثَنَا سُلَيْمَانُ بْنُ عَبْدِ الرَّحْمَنِ الدِّمَشْقِيُّ قَالَ حَدَّثَنَا الْوَلِيدُ بْنُ مُسْلِمٍ قَالَ حَدَّثَنَا جُرَيْجٌ عَنْ عَطَاءِ بْنِ أَبِي رَبَّاحٍ وَعِكْرِمَةُ مَوْلَى بْنِ عَبَّاسٍ عَنْ ابْنِ عَبَّاسٍ قَالَ: بَيْنَمَا نَحْنُ عِنْدَ رَسُولِ اللهِ ﷺ إِذْ جَاءَهُ عَلِيُّ بْنُ أَبِي طَالِبٍ فَقَالَ: بِأَبِي أَنْتَ وَأُمِّي تَفَلَّتَ هَذَا الْقُرآنُ مِنْ صَدْرِي فَمَا أَجِدُنِي أَقْدِرُ عَلَيْهِ فَقَالَ لَهُ رَسُولُ اللهِ ﷺ(٢٧): «يَا أَبَا الْحَسَنِ أَفَلَا أُعَلِّمُكَ كَلِمَاتٍ يَنْفَعُكَ اللهُ بِهِنَّ، وَيَنْفَعُ بِهِنَّ مَنْ عَلَّمْتَهُ، وَيُثَبِّتُ مَا تَعَلَّمْتَ فِي صَدْرِكَ؟ قَالَ: أَجَلْ يَا رَسُولَ اللهِ فَعَلِّمْنِي، قَالَ: إِذَا كَانَ لَيْلَةَ الْجُمُعَةِ فَإِنْ اسْتَطَعْتَ أَنْ تَقُومَ فِي ثُلُثِ اللَّيْلِ الْآخِرِ فَإِنَّهَا سَاعَةٌ مَشْهُودَةٌ وَالدُّعَاءُ فِيهَا مُسْتَجَابٌ، وَقَدْ قَالَ أَخِي يَعْقُوبُ لِبَنِيهِ ﴿سَوْفَ أَسْتَغْفِرُ لَكُمْ رَبِّي﴾ يَقُولُ حَتَّى تَأْتِي لَيْلَةُ الْجُمُعَةِ، فَإِنْ لَمْ تَسْتَطِعْ فَقُمْ فِي وَسَطِهَا فَإِنْ لَمْ تَسْتَطِعْ فَقُمْ فِي أَوَّلِهَا، فَصَلِّ أَرْبَعَ رَكَعَاتٍ تَقْرَأُ فِي الرَّكْعَةِ الْأُولَى بِفَاتِحَةِ الْكِتَابِ وَسُورَةِ يَس، وَفِي الرَّكْعَةِ الثَّانِيَةِ: بِفَاتِحَةِ الْكِتَابِ وَحم - الدُّخَانِ - وَفِي الرَّكْعَةِ الثَّالِثَةِ: بِفَاتِحَةِ الْكِتَابِ وَالَمْ تَنْزِيلُ - السَّجْدَةِ - وَفِي الرَّكْعَةِ الرَّابِعَةِ: بِفَاتِحَةِ الْكِتَابِ وَتَبَارَكَ الْمُفَصَّلِ يَعْنِي تَبَارَكَ (الملك) - فَإِذَا فَرَغْتَ مِنَ التَّشَهُّدِ فَاحْمَدِ اللهَ

---

٢٧) أخرجه الترمذي في سننه ٥/٥٦٣ برقم ٣٥٧٠ عن ابن عباس - ط / الحلبي. وذكره في إتحاف السادة المتقين ٥/٣٢ وعزاه للحاكم والطبرى عن ابن عباس ـ ط / دار الكتب العلمية. وذكره ابن كثير في ذيل تفسيره وعزاه للطيران في الكبير - ط / الحلى.

seeing what pleases You. O Allah, Originator of the Heavens and the Earth, Possessor of Majesty and Honour, keep my heart steadfast in preserving Your Book as You have taught me, and grant me the ability to recite it in a manner pleasing to You. O Allah, Originator of the Heavens and the Earth, Possessor of Majesty, Honour, and Power that is not opposed, I ask You, O Allah, O Merciful One, by Your Majesty and the light of Your countenance, to enlighten my sight with Your Book, to loosen my tongue with it, to expand my heart with it, to open my chest with it, and to make my body act upon it. Indeed, none can help me attain the truth but You, and none can bring it except You, and there is no power nor might except with Allah, the Most-High and the Most-Great.'

Then the Prophet Muhammad ﷺ said: 'O Abū al-Ḥasan, do this on Friday night, either three, five, or seven times, and, by the permission of Allah, your supplication will be answered.'" Ibn ʿAbbās said: "By Allah, ʿAlī did not stay [engaged in this practice] for more than three or seven sessions until the Messenger of Allah came upon him in a similar gathering. ʿAlī said: 'O Messenger of Allah, while alone, I could not recite more than four verses or the like, and when I recited them, they would slip away from me. But today, I have learned 40 verses or the like, and when I recite them, it is as if the Book of Allah is right before my eyes. Indeed, I used to forget the Hadiths, but now when I desire to recall them, they do not slip away from me.' At that moment, the Messenger of Allah ﷺ said to him: 'A believer, by the Lord of the Kaʿbah, O Abu al-Hasan.'" This is a *ḥasan gharīb* Hadith, transmitted uniquely through the narration of al-Walīd ibn Muslim.

وَأَحسِنِ الثَّنَاءَ عَلَى اللهِ وَصَلِّ عَلَيَّ وَأَحسِنْ وَعَلَى سَائِرِ النَّبِيِّينَ وَاسْتَغْفِرْ لِلْمُؤْمِنِينَ وَالْمُؤْمِنَاتِ وَلِإِخْوَانِكَ الَّذِينَ سَبَقُوكَ بِالْإِيمَانِ. **ثُمَّ قُلْ فِي آخِرِ ذَلِكَ**: اللَّهُمَّ ارْحَمْنِي بِتَرْكِ الْمَعَاصِي أَبَداً مَا أَبْقَيْتَنِي وَارْحَمْنِي أَنْ أَتَكَلَّفَ مَا لَا يَعْنِينِي وَارْزُقْنِي حُسْنَ النَّظَرِ فِيمَا يُرْضِيكَ عَنِّي. اللَّهُمَّ بَدِيعَ السَّمَوَاتِ وَالْأَرْضِ ذِي الجَلَالِ وَالإِكْرَامِ الْزِمْ قَلْبِي حِفْظَ كِتَابِكَ كَمَا عَلَّمْتَنِي وَارْزُقْنِي أَنْ أَتْلُوهُ عَلَى النَّحوِ الَّذِي يُرْضِيكَ، اللَّهُمَّ بَدِيعَ السَّمَوَاتِ وَالْأَرْضِ ذَا الْجَلَالِ وَالْإِكْرَامِ وَالْعِزَّةِ الَّتِي لَا تُرَامُ أَسأَلُكَ يَا اللهُ يَا رَحْمنُ بِجَلَالِكَ وَنُورِ وَجْهِكَ أَنْ تُنَوِّرَ بِكِتَابِكَ بَصَرِي، وَأَنْ تُطْلِقَ بِهِ لِسَانِي، وَأَنْ تُفْرِجَ بِهِ عَنْ قَلْبِي، وَأَنْ تَشْرَحَ بِهِ صَدْرِي، وَتُعْمِلَ بِهِ بَدَنِي فَإِنَّهُ لَا يُعِينُنِي عَلَى الْحَقِّ غَيْرُكَ وَلَا يَأْتِيهِ إِلَّا أَنْتَ وَلَا حَوْلَ وَلَا قُوَّةَ إِلَّا بِاللهِ الْعَلِيِّ الْعَظِيمِ) «يَا أَبَا الْحَسَنِ تَفْعَلُ ذَلِكَ ثَلَاثَ جُمَعٍ أَوْ خَمْساً أَوْ سَبْعاً تُجَابُ بِإِذْنِ اللهِ تَعَالَى، وَالَّذِي بَعَثَنِي بِالْحَقِّ مَا أَخْطَأَ مُؤْمِناً قَطُّ. (قَالَ ابْنُ عَبَّاسٍ: فَوَاللهِ مَا لَبِثَ عَلِيٌّ إِلَّا خَمْساً أَوْ سَبْعاً حَتَّى جَاءَ رَسُولُ اللهِ فِي مِثْلِ ذَلِكَ الْمَجلِسِ فَقَالَ يَا رَسُولَ اللهِ: إِنِّي كُنْتُ فِيمَا خَلَا لَا آخُذُ إِلَّا أَرْبَعَ آيَاتٍ وَنَحْوَهُنَّ فَإِذَا قَرَأْتُهُنَّ تَفَلَّتْنَ وَأَنَا أَتَعَلَّمُ الْيَوْمَ أَرْبَعِينَ آيَةً أَوْ نَحْوَهَا فَإِذَا قَرَأْتُهُنَّ عَلَى نَفْسِي فَكَأَنَّمَا كِتَابُ اللهِ بَيْنَ عَيْنَيَّ وَلَقَدْ كُنْتُ أَسْمَعُ الْحَدِيثَ فَإِذَا أَرَدْتُهُ تَفَلَّتَ وَأَنَا الْيَوْمَ أَسْمَعُ الْأَحَادِيثَ فَإِذَا تَحَدَّثْتُ بِهَا لَمْ أُخْرِمْ مِنْهَا حَرْفاً فَقَالَ لَهُ رَسُولُ اللهِ ﷺ عِنْدَ ذَلِكَ: «مُؤْمِنٌ وَرَبِّ الْكَعْبَةِ يَا أَبَا الْحَسَنِ». هَذَا حَدِيثٌ حَسَنٌ غَرِيبٌ لَا نَعْرِفُهُ إِلَّا مِنْ حَدِيثِ الْوَلِيدِ بْنِ مُسْلِمٍ.

A Benefit for Treating Forgetfulness from the Litanies of the Righteous

The Imam, the knower of Allah, Sheikh Aḥmad ibn ʿĪsā Aḥmad ibn ʿĪsā, known as Zarrūq al-Maghribī, mentioned in his commentary on the poetic composition of the beautiful names of Allah – authored by Imam Nūr al-Dīn al-Dimyāṭī ﷺ – at the verse:

"O Protector of faith, grant me a secure submission,
And a deep covering, O Protector, who makes paths clear."[46]

"The one who consistently recites this verse will strengthen their memory, eliminate forgetfulness, and attain truth, affirmation, and obedience."

Additionally, Sīdī Aḥmad ibn Zarrūq – may Allah sanctify his secret –mentioned in his aforementioned commentary at the verse of the poet:

"O Ever-Living, remove the death of my heart,
For as long as You are facilitating, I am sustained."[47]

"When the dull-witted person recites it sixteen times in an empty place, Allah will secure them from the afflictions of forgetfulness, strengthen their memory, and illuminate their heart."

---

46 *Majmūʿah Laṭīfah Tashtamilu ʿalā Daʿwah al-Jaljalawtiyyah wa al-Dumyāṭiyyah wa al-Burhutiyyah*, p. 20, Maktabah Dār al-Saʿdiyyah.

47 *Majmūʿah Laṭīfah Tashtamilu ʿalā Daʿwah al-Jaljalawtiyyah wa al-Dumyāṭiyyah wa al-Burhutiyyah*, p. 24, Maktabah Dār al-Saʿdiyyah.

فَائِدَةٌ لِعِلَاجِ النِّسيَانِ مِنْ أَوْرَادِ الصَّالِحِينَ

وَقَدْ ذَكَرَ الْإِمَامُ الْعَارِفُ بِاللهِ تَعَالَى الشَّيْخُ أَحْمَدُ بْنُ عِيسَى الشَّهِيرُ بِزَرُّوقٍ الْمَغْرِبِيِّ فِي شَرْحِهِ عَلَى نَظْمِ الْأَسْمَاءِ الْحُسْنَى الَّتِي نَظَمَهَا الْإِمَامُ نُورُ الدِّينِ الدُّمْيَاطِيُّ رَحِمَهُ اللهُ تَعَالَى عِنْدَ قَوْلِهِ فِي النَّظْمِ:

وَيَا مُؤْمِنُ هَبْ لِي أَمَاناً مُسْلَماً

وَسِتْراً عَمِيقاً يَا مُهَيْمِنُ مُسْبَلاً (٢٨)

قَالَ مَنْ دَاوَمَ عَلَى هَذَا الْبَيْتِ قَوِيَ حِفْظُهُ وَذَهَبَ نِسْيَانُهُ وَحَصَلَ لَهُ الصِّدْقُ وَالتَّصْدِيقُ وَالْإِذْعَانُ وَذَكَرَ أَيْضاً سَيِّدِي أَحْمَدُ بْنُ زَرُّوقٍ قَدَّسَ اللهُ سِرَّهُ فِي شَرْحِهِ الْمَذْكُورِ عِنْدَ قَوْلِ النَّاظِمِ:

وَيَا حَيُّ أَذْهِبْ مَوْتَ قَلْبِي فَلَمْ أَزَلْ

بِذِكْرِكَ يَا قَيُّومُ مَا دُمْتَ مَوْصِلاً (٢٩)

قَالَ: وَإِذَا قَرَأَهَا الْبَلِيدُ سِتَّةَ عَشَرَ مَرَّةً فِي مَكَانٍ خَالِي فَإِنَّ اللهَ يُؤَمِّنُهُ مِنْ عَوَارِضِ النِّسْيَانِ وَيُقَوِّي حِفْظَهُ وَيُنَوِّرُ قَلْبَهُ.

---

٢٨) انظر مجموعة لطيفة تشتمل على دعوة الجلجلوتية والدمياطية والبرهتية ص ٢٠ ط / المكتبة السعدية

٢٩) انظر مجموعة لطيفة تشتمل على دعوة الجلجلوتية والدمياطية والبرهتية من ٢٤ ط / المكتبة السعدية.

Chapter 4 - Treatments Used for Memory Retention

This chapter pertains to treatments used for memory retention and the removal of forgetfulness as mentioned by physicians, along with tangible remedies.

* * *

You should know that divine treatments derived from Quranic verses, Prophetic traditions, and the reports of righteous individuals concerning forgetfulness and other matters are more deserving of priority over material remedies cited in medical books. It is imperative for individuals to originally treat themselves with spiritual and religious therapies, such as supplications and invocations mentioned in that regard. As such, they should defer the use of material remedies mentioned in medicinal books. They should utilize what is mentioned in the latter subsequently, as this approach is more complete in terms of religious etiquette and more successful for the one being guided in the desired action. Healing and the disappearance of adversities opposing the body depend entirely upon Allah.

* * *

This is the entirety of medical treatments as mentioned by the chief Abū ʿAlī ibn Sīnā ﷺ in his book *al-Qānūn*, where he said: "In the treatments for the corruption of memory, which is forgetfulness after mentioning, the reasons for that, and that forgetfulness can be due to heat, dryness, or moisture, as we have previously presented." He said: "The comparison between heat and dryness is easier in treatment and dealing with what was mentioned before than in the treatment of wakefulness and insomnia."

He said: "By avoiding the bathhouse because it yields a bad mixture, and one must avoid thinking, intercourse, and play, and use calmness and rest, and maintain the moistening of the head with rose oil, abundant vinegar, and watercress, pomegranate, and yoghurt on the head,

الْفَصْلُ الرَّابِعُ

يَتَعَلَّقُ بِأَدْوِيَةِ الْحِفْظِ وَإِزَالَةِ آفَةِ النِّسْيَانِ مِمَّا ذَكَرَهُ الْأَطِبَّاءُ وَمِنَ الدَّوَاءِ الْمَحْسُوسِ اِعْلَمْ أَنَّ الْأَدْوِيَةَ الْإِلَهِيَّةَ الرَّبَّانِيَّةَ الْمُسْتَفَادَةَ مِنَ الْآيَاتِ الْقُرْآنِيَّةِ وَالْأَحَادِيثِ النَّبَوِيَّةِ وَكَلَامِ الصَّالِحِينَ مِنَ الْأَخْبَارِ فِي حَقِّ النِّسْيَانِ وَغَيْرِهِ أَوْلَى بِالتَّقْدِيمِ عَلَى الْأَدْوِيَةِ الْمَحْسُوسَةِ الْمَذْكُورَةِ فِي كُتُبِ الطِّبِّ وَيَنْبَغِي لِلْإِنْسَانِ أَنْ يُعَالِجَ نَفْسَهُ أَوَّلًا بِالْمُعَالِجَاتِ الْمَعْنَوِيَّةِ الْإِلَهِيَّةِ كَالْأَدْعِيَةِ وَالْأَذْكَارِ الْوَارِدَةِ فِي ذَلِكَ وَيُؤَخِّرُ الْمُعَالَجَةَ الْمَحْسُوسَةَ الْوَارِدَةَ فِي كُتُبِ الطِّبِّ ثُمَّ يَسْتَعْمِلُ مَا وَرَدَ فِي كُتُبِ الطِّبِّ بَعْدَ ذَلِكَ فَإِنَّ هَذَا الصَّنِيعَ أَكْمَلُ فِي الْأَدَبِ الشَّرْعِيِّ وَأَنْجَحُ لِلْمَقْودِ فِي الْأَمْرِ الْمَرْعِيِّ وَعَلَى اللهِ حُصُولُ الشِّفَاءِ وَزَوَالُ الْآفَاتِ الْمُعَارِضَةِ بِالْجِسْمِ لَهَا وَالْاِنْتِفَاءُ فَهَذِهِ جُمْلَةُ الْمُعَالِجَاتِ الطِّبِّيَةِ مَا ذَكَرَهُ الرَّئِيسُ أَبُو عَلِيِّ بْنُ سِينَا رَحِمَهُ اللهُ تَعَالَى فِي كِتَابِهِ الْقَانُونِ فِي عِلْمِ الطِّبِّ حَيْثُ قَالَ[٣٠]: فِي مُعَالِجَاتِ فَسَادِ الذِّكْرِ وَهُوَ النِّسْيَانُ بَعْدَ ذِكْرِهِ أَسْبَابَ ذَلِكَ وَأَنَّ النِّسْيَانَ قَدْ يَكُونُ عَنْ حَرٍّ وَيُبْسٍ وَقَدْ يَكُونُ عَنْ بَرْدٍ وَرُطُوبَةٍ كَمَا قَدَّمْنَا فَقَالَ: الْمُقَارِنُ لِلْحَرِّ وَالْيُبْسِ فَهُوَ أَسْهَلُ عِلَاجاً وَمُعَالَجَةً بِمَا ذَكَرَهُ قَبْلَ ذَلِكَ فِي مُعَالَجَةِ الْيَقَظَةِ وَالسَّهَرِ. حَيْثُ قَالَ بِاجْتِنَابِ الْحَمَّامِ فَإِنَّهُ يُثِيرُ أَخْلَاطاً رَدِيئَةً وَيَجِبُ أَنْ يَهْجُرَ الْفِكْرَ وَالْجِمَاعَ وَاللَّعِبَ وَيَسْتَعْمِلَ السُّكُونَ

٣٠) انظر القانون لابن سينا ٣/٥٠ - ط. بولاق

and prolonging with heated water which contains sedge, centipede, and thorn, and the softening of the head with milk fat, musk fat, and costus oil with centipede, and inhaling perfumes, using them, and dripping them into the ear, especially nilofer. Its snuff form may be used whereby it is placed under the foot. As for forgetfulness that occurs due to dryness, then the patient must be nourished with moderately moist foods and use exercises towards the head with massage and being immersed within a coarse cloth, moving the hands and legs, and perhaps even being ironed like the two irons."

* * *

Pomegranate and milk on the head, along with long drenches in water that is infused with celery, rosemary, and basil, are necessary. Additionally, one should apply butter and musk oil, along with storax, to the head, and inhale and apply various perfumes and essential oils, especially nilofer, under the feet. As for forgetfulness caused by a dry and moist substance, it should be treated with the least invasive means, such as hand massages and applying antelope fat and storax. Thenceforth, the patient should transition to more potent treatments, such as using the medications prescribed by physicians and resources referred to in medicine books.

If the forgetfulness arises from cold and moisture, it should be purged with less invasive purgatives such as aloe vera and hyssop. They can then gradually move to more intense treatments like the use of sedge, centipede, and thorn. Finally, if the patient is believed to suffer from severe imbalances, the use of bile paste should be considered, as it is the strongest substance for strengthening the mind. However, caution must be exercised in this to prevent excessive drying, which can exacerbate forgetfulness. The patient should also avoid excessive light and abstain from alcohol and excessive sexual activity.

* * *

In cases of heat, caution is warranted due to its adverse effects on the sensitive spirit. But should it be deemed necessary, the patient should

وَالرَّاحَةَ وَإِدَامَةَ تَعْرِيقِ الرَّأْسِ بِدَهْنِ الْوَرْدِ وَالْخَلِّ الْكَثِيرِ وَمَاءِ الْحِصْرِمِ) [٣١] وَالرُّمَّانِ وَحَلْبَ اللَّبَنِ عَلَى الرَّأْسِ وَالْمَنْطُولَاتُ بِالْمِيَاهِ الْمَطْبُوخِ فِيهَا سَذَبٌ وَجَنْدَبِيدَ سِتْرٍ وَحَاقِدٍ تَرَبُّحًا وَتَرْمِيخُ الرَّأْسِ بِدَهْنِ الْبَانِ وَدَهْنِ الْمِسْكِ وَدَهْنِ الْقَسْطِ مَعَ جَنْدَبِيدِ سِتْرٍ وَاسْتِنْشَاقُ الْأَدْهَانِ وَإِسْعَاطُهَا وَتَقْطِيرُهَا فِي الْأُذُنِ خُصُوصاً النَّيْلُوفِرُ لَا سِيَّمَا سُعُوطاً وَذَلِكَ أَسْفَلَ الْقَدَمِ بِهَا وَأَمَّا النِّسْيَانُ الْكَائِنُ عَنْ يُبْسٍ مُجَرَّدٍ فَيَجِبُ فِيهِ أَنْ يُغَذَّى الْعَلِيلُ بِالْأَغْذِيَةِ الرَّطْبَةِ الْمُعْتَدِلَةِ وَأَنْ يَسْتَعْمِلَ رِيَاضَةً نَاحِيَةَ الرَّأْسِ بِالدَّلْكِ وَالْعمر بِالْخِرْقَةِ الْخَشِنَةِ وَتَحْرِيكِ الْيَدَيْنِ وَالرِّجْلَيْنِ وَرُبَّمَا احْتَاجَ إِلَى أَنْ يُكْوَى كَيَّتَيْنِ [٣٢] خَلْفَ الْقَفَا وَيَسْتَعْمِلَ مِيَاهًا طُبِخَ فِيهَا بَابُونَجٌ وَإِكْلِيلُ الْمَلِكِ وَكَرَعَانُ الْمَاعِزِ وَمِنَ الْأَدْهَانِ دَهْنُ السَّوْسَنِ وَالنَّرْجِسِ وَالْخِيَرِى وَأَمَّا إِذَا كَانَ النِّسْيَانُ عَنْ مَادَّةٍ ذَاتِ بَرْدٍ وَرُطُوبَةٍ فَلْيَسْتَفْرِغْهُ بِالْاِسْتِفْرَاغَاتِ الَّتِي أَخَفُّ مِثْلُ الْأَيَادِجِ وَشَحْمُ الْحَنْظَلِ وَجَنْدَبِيدُ سِتْرٍ ثُمَّ يُدْرِجُ إِلَى الْأَيَادِجَاتِ الْكِبَارِ ثُمَّ يَسْتَعْمِلُ إِنْ آمَنَ سُوءَ الْمِزَاجِ الْحَادِّ مَعْجُونَ الْبَلَادِرِ فَإِنَّهُ أَقْوَى شَيْءٍ فِي تَقْوِيَةِ الذِّهْنِ وَلْيَحْذَرْ أَنْ يَبْلُغَ فِي التَّخْفِيفِ إِلَى إِفْنَاءِ الرُّطُوبَاتِ الْأَصْلِيَّةِ فَتَبِعَهَا بَرْدُ الْمِزَاجِ وَذَلِكَ مِمَّا يَزِيدُ فِي النِّسْيَانِ وَلْيَسْكُنْ بَيْتاً كَثِيرَ الضَّوْءِ وَيَجِبُ أَنْ يَجْتَنِبَ الْمُسْكِرَاتِ

---

٣١) الحصرم: هو عصير العنب الأخضر

٣٢) لما ورد عن جابر أن النبي الله قال: « الشفاء في ثلاثة (شربة عسل، وشرطة محجم، وكيسة بنار) [أخرجه مسلم ٤/٧٢٩ - ط. دار الحديث] والكية موضع الكي ونحوه يكويه كما أحرق جلده بحديدة ونحوها وهي المكواه وهو المقصود هنا انظر - القاموس المحيط (٤ / ٣٧٦).

bathe in lukewarm water. Afterwards, gentle management should be applied, and excess water should be avoided. Additionally, excessive sleep, especially after overeating, should be avoided, since it weakens the temperament and encourages drowsiness. Sleeping too much fills the brain with vapour, worsening forgetfulness.

It has been observed that certain remedies, such as preserving jams and pepper, increase memory retention considerably. These treatments involve consuming specific quantities of herbs and spices on a daily basis, accompanied by the application of various oils and honey. It is necessary to maintain a suitable environment with proper lighting to achieve optimal results. These remedies and their explanations are extensively discussed in medical references and books.

وَمَهَابَّ الرِّيَاحِ وَالْإِمْتِلَاءِ وَيَجْتَنِبَ الْإِغْتِسَالَ بِالْمَاءِ أَصْلاً. أَمَّا الْحَارُّ فَلِمَا فِيهِ مِنَ الْإِدْخَالِ فَلِمَا يُحْذَرُ وَيَضُرُّ بِالرُّوحِ الْحَاسِّ وَأَقُولُ: لَعَلَّهُ إِذَا دَعَتِ الضَّرُورَةُ إِلَى ذَلِكَ فَلْيَغْتَسِلْ بِمَاءٍ مُعْتَدِلٍ لَا حَارٍّ وَلَا بَارِدٍ ثُمَّ قَالَ فِي الْقَانُونِ: فَإِنْ عَرَضَ لَهُ الْإِمْتِلَاءُ لُطْفَ التَّدْبِيرِ بَعْدَهُ وَالْإِسْتِكْثَارُ مِنْ اِسْتِعْمَالِ الْمَاءِ آخِرُ شَيْءٍ لَهُ وَالْقَيْلُولَةُ الْكَثِيرَةُ وَبِالْجُمْلَةِ النَّوْمُ الْكَثِيرُ ضَارًّا لَهُ وَخُصُوصاً عَلَى اِمْتِلَاءٍ كَثِيرٍ وَالْإِفْرَاطُ مِنَ السَّهَرِ أَيْضاً يُضْعِفُ الرُّوحَ وَيُحَلُّهُ وَمَعَ ذَلِكَ فَيَمْلَأُ الدِّمَاغَ بَخْرُهُ وَقَدْ جُرِّبَ لِهَذَا النَّوْعِ مِنَ النِّسْيَانِ أُلُوجُ الْمُرَبَّى وَالدَّارُ فُلْفُلِ الْمُرَبَّى وَوُجِدَا أَنَّهُمَا يَزِيدَانِ الْحِفْظَ زِيَادَةً بَيِّنَةً وَقَدْ جُرِّبَ هَذَا الدَّوَاءُ وَصِفَتُهُ يُؤْخَذُ كُنْدُرٌ وَسَعْدٌ وَفُلْفُلٌ أَبْيَضُ وَزَعْفَرَانٌ وَمُرٌّ جُزْءٌ بِعَسَلٍ مُجْزٍ وَتَنَاوَلْ كُلَّ يَوْمٍ وَزْنَ دِرْهَمٍ وَاحِدٍ وَجُرِّبَ أَيْضاً وَنُسْخَتُهُ يُؤْخَذُ فُلْفُلٌ وَكَمُّونٌ جُزْءَانِ وَسُكَّرٌ وَطَبَرْزَدٌ ثَلَاثَةُ أَجْزَاءٍ وَجَرَّبَهُ أَيْضاً كُلَّ يَوْمٍ عَلَى الرِّيقِ يُسْتَعْمَلُ مِثْقَالٌ فِيهِ مِنَ الْكُنْدُرِ ثَلَاثَةُ أَرْبَاعٍ وَمِنَ الْفُلْفُلِ رُبْعٌ وَأَيْضاً مِنَ الْكَمُّونِ خِمْسًتَا جُزْءًا وَمِنَ الْفُلْفُلِ جُزْءٌ وَاحِدٌ وَمِنَ السَّعْدِ اِثْنَانِ وَمِنَ الْإِهْلِيلَجِ الْأَسْوَدِ اِثْنَانِ وَمِنْ عَسَلِ الْبَلَادِرِ وَاحِدٌ وَمِنْ عَسَلِ النَّحْلِ ضِعْفُ الْجَمِيعِ وَيَجِبُ أَنْ يَكُونَ مَسْكَنٌ مِثْلُهُ بَيْتاً فِيهِ الضَّوْءُ وَقَدْ أَطَالَ الْأَطِبَّاءُ فِي بَيَانِ ذَلِكَ وَأَدْوِيَتِهِ وَمَرْجِعُهُ كُتُبُ الطِّبِّ.

Chapter 5 - On Legal Rulings

With regard to the legal rulings arising from forgetfulness, the ʿAllāmah Ibn Mālik stated in his explanation of *al-Manār* in the fundamentals of jurisprudence: "Forgetfulness does not preclude one's obligation with respect to the rights of Allah ﷻ. Thus, if one misses a prayer due to forgetfulness, the obligation does not drop, and the individual is required to make up for it. However, it is different if forgetfulness overtakes one, such as in fasting, whereby it overwhelms a person due to the fact that the soul is naturally inclined towards eating and drinking, which is why the most common cause of it (forgetfulness) is in fasting. The same is said for forgetting to recite the *tasmiyah* when sacrificing; this is because sacrificing animals causes apprehension and fear, due to one's natural fear of it; thus, a person's demeanour changes leading to frequent forgetfulness of the *tasmiyah*. Likewise, when a person forgetfully recites the *salām* in the first sitting; because it is the place of the *salām*, forgetfulness often occurs there. In all these cases, such lapses are excused because [in those cases] forgetfulness proceeds by way of the Owner of the Right, without the slave having any choice in it. However, forgetfulness is never an excuse with regard to the rights of the servants [of Allah]. This is such that if he were to destroy the possessions of someone else, he is required to repay their value."

The author of *Sharḥ Mirqāt al-Wuṣūl* said, "Forgetfulness does not negate any obligation because the full intellectual capacity remains. Nor is it an excuse with regard to the rights of people, because they are respected due to their need of them, not as a Divine test.[48] And this neediness of theirs is not removed by forgetfulness. Thus, if someone were to destroy someone else's property, forgetfully, he is still obligated to pay for it."

Likewise, it is not considered an excuse in the case of His ﷻ right if the forgetfulness is because of the servant's neglectfulness. In other

---

48 Translator's note: This means that the Divine rights are a test only because God does not need our acts of obedience. Rather, we are the only ones that benefit by undertaking acts of obedience. But with respect to the creation, they are in need of their property, and therefore their rights are not overlooked due to someone's forgetfulness.

الْفَصْلُ الْخَامِسُ

فِي الْأَحْكَامِ الشَّرْعِيَّةِ الْمُتَرَتِّبَةِ عَلَى النِّسْيَانِ قَالَ الْعَلَّامَةُ ابْنُ مَلَكٍ فِي)شَرْحِهِ عَلَى الْمَنَارِ(فِي أُصُولِ الْفِقْهِ: وَالنِّسْيَانُ لَا يُنَافِي الْوُجُوبَ فِي حَقِّ اللهِ تَعَالَى فَإِنْ فَاتَتِ الصَّلَاةُ عَنِ الْمُكَلَّفِ بِالنِّسْيَانِ لَا يَسْقُطُ الْوُجُوبُ عَنْهُ وَيَلْزَمُهُ الْقَضَاءُ لَكِنَّ النِّسْيَانَ إِذَا كَانَ غَالِباً كَمَا فِي الصَّوْمِ فَإِنَّهُ غَالِبٌ فِيهِ لِأَنَّ النَّفْسَ مَائِلَةٌ طَبْعاً إِلَى الْأَكْلِ وَالشَّرَابِ فَأَوْجَبُ ذَلِكَ نِسْيَانُ الصَّوْمِ وَالتَّسْمِيَةِ فِي الذَبِيحَةِ فإِنَّ ذبحَ الْحَيَوَانِ يُوجِبَ هَيْبَتَهُ وَخوْفاً لِنفُورِ الطَّبْع مِنْهُ وَيَتَغَيَّرُ منه حَالُ الْبَشَرِ فَتَكْثُرُ الْغَفْلَةُ عَنِ التَّسْمِيَّةِ فِي تِلْكَ الْحَالَةِ لِإِشْتِغَالِ قَلْبِهِ بِالْخَوْفِ وَسَلَامُ النَّاسِي فِي الْقَعْدَةُ الْأُولَى فَيَكْثُرُ النِّسْيَانُ فِيهِ يكون عَفْواً لِأَنَّ النِّسْيَانَ مِنْ جِهَةِ صَاحِبِ الْحَقِّ بِلَا اِخْتِيَارٍ لِلْعَبْدِ فِيهِ وَلَا يَجْعَلُ النِّسْيَانُ عُذْراً فِي حُقُوقِ الْعِبَادِ حَتَّى لَوْ أَتْلَفَ مَالَ إِنْسَانٍ نَاسِياً يَجِبُ عَلَيْهِ الضَّمَانُ وَقَالَ فِي (شَرْحِ مِرْقَاةِ الْوُصُولِ): وَالنِّسْيَانُ لَيْسَ مُنَافِياً لِلْوُجُوبِ لِبَقَاءِ الْقُدْرَةِ لِكَمَالِ الْعَقْلِ وَلَا عُذْرَ فِي حُقُوقِ الْعِبَادِ لِأَنَّهَا محترمة لِحَاجَتِهِمْ لَا لِلْاِبْتِلَاءِ بِالنِّسْيَانِ لَا يُفَوِّتُ هَذَا الْاِحْتِرَامَ فَلَوْ أَتْلَفَ مَالَ إِنْسَانٍ نَاسِياً يَجِبُ عَلَيْهِ الضَّمَانُ وَكَذَا لَا يَكُونُ عُذْراً فِي حَقِّهِ تَعَالَى إِنْ قَصَّرَ الْعَبْدُ أَيْ وَقَعَ الْعَبْدُ فِي النِّسْيَانِ بِالتَّقْصِيرِ مِنْهُ كَالْأَكْلِ فِي الصَّلَاةِ حَيْثُ لَمْ يَتَذَكَّرْ مَعَ وُجُودِ الْمُذَكِّرِ وَهُوَ هَيْئَةُ الصَّلَاةِ فَلَا يَكُونُ عُذْراً. وَإِلَّا، أَيْ وَإِنْ لَمْ يَقَعْ فِيهِ بِتَقْصِيرِهِ فَعُذْرُهُ مُطْلَقٌ أَيْ سَوَاءٌ كَانَ مَعَهُ مَا: يَكُونُ دَاعِياً إِلَى النِّسْيَانِ وَمُنَافِياً لِلتَّذَكُّرِ كَالْأَكْلِ فِي الصَّوْمِ لِمَا فِي الطَّبِيعَةِ مِنَ الشَّوْقِ إِلَى الْأَكْلِ وَلَمْ يَكُنْ

words, if the servant treats his obligation lightly, such as if he were to eat in the prayer, not remembering [that he is praying] despite the fact that there is an invoker of Divine remembrance, which is the form of the prayer, he would not be excused. Otherwise, if it did not occur due to his neglectfulness, then he has an unrestricted excuse, regardless of whether he is affected by something innate to him that causes forgetfulness and prevents his remembrance, such as eating while one is fasting. That is because one's natural disposition has a strong inclination towards food. And his excuse also stands if he is not affected by such a condition, such as leaving the *basmalāh* while performing the ritual sacrifice. In that case, there is no natural inclination towards it. Nor is there anything to remind him to have it in mind and to pronounce it with the tongue.

It is for this reason that forgetfully giving the *salām* in the first sitting is excused to the point that it does not invalidate one's prayer, because it is not neglectfulness on the part of the person. After all, forgetfulness is [at times] unavoidable in that position due to the frequency of the *taslīm* of the one who is praying in the sitting position. It is that very position which prompts the *taslīm*.

Ibn Nujaym stated in *al-Ashbāh wa al-Naẓā'ir*:

> "Regarding the rulings of forgetfulness: Scholars unanimously agree that forgetfulness absolves one from sin entirely due to the authentic Hadith: 'Allah has pardoned my Ummah for mistakes, forgetfulness, and what they are coerced to do.' The scholars of the fundamentals of the religion have pronounced that this statement is to be interpreted metaphorically through the indications of what is being discussed. That is because the actual error and its accompanying factors are not removed. Thus, the meaning is that its corresponding ruling is lifted. And its ruling is of different categories: 1) Otherworldly, which is a sin, and 2) worldly, which is corruption. The two rulings are different. Thus, the sin, after it has been committed, becomes a metaphorical homonym. Consequently, it is not universal. As for our reasoning, it is because a homonym is never universal. Accordingly, if the otherworldly nature of it is established through consensus, the other [worldly nature] is also established through consensus, as mentioned in *al-Tanqīḥ*. And we have discussed it in full in our

كَتَرْكِ التَّسْمِيَةِ عِنْدَ الذَّبْحِ فَإِنَّهُ لَا أَدْعَى إِلَى تَرْكِهَا لَكِنْ لَيْسَ هُنَاكَ مَا يُذَكِّرُ إِحْضَارَهَا بِالْبَالِ وَإِجْرَاءَهَا عَلَى اللِّسَانِ فَسَلَامُ الناسي فِي الْقَعْدَةِ يَكُونُ عُذْراً حَتَّى لَا يُبْطِلُ صَلَاتَهُ إِذْ لَا تَقْصِيرَ مِنْ جِهَتِهِ فَالنِّسْيَانُ غَالِبٌ فِي تِلْكَ الْحَالَةِ لِكَثْرَةِ تَسْلِيمِ الْمُصَلِّي فِي الْقَعْدَةِ فَهِيَ دَاعِيَةٌ إِلَى السَّلَامِ وَقَالَ الْعَلَّامَةُ ابْنُ نَجِيمٍ فِي كِتَابِ (الْأَشْبَاهِ وَالنَّظَائِرِ) (٣٣) فِي أَحْكَامِ النِّسْيَانِ: وَاتَّفَقَ الْعُلَمَاءُ عَلَى أَنَّهُ مُسْقِطٌ لِلْإِثْمِ مُطْلَقاً لِلْحَدِيثِ الْحَسَنِ (أَنَّ اللّٰهَ وَضَعَ عَنْ أُمَّتِي الْخَطَأَ وَالنِّسْيَانَ وَمَا اسْتُكْرِهُوا عَلَيْهِ) (٣٤) قَالَ الْأُصُولِيُّونَ: إِنَّهُ مِنْ بَابِ تَرْكِهِ الْحَقِيقَةَ بِدَلَالَةِ مَحَلِّ الْكَلَامِ لِأَنَّ عَيْنَ الْخَطَإِ وَأَخَوَيْهِ غَيْرُ مَرْفُوعٍ فَالْمُرَادُ حُكْمُهَا وَهُوَ أَنْوَاعٌ أُخْرَوِيٌّ وَهُوَ الْإِثْمُ وَدُنْيَوِيٌّ وَهُوَ الْفَسَادُ وَالْحُكْمَانِ مُخْتَلِفَانِ فَصَارَ الْإِثْمُ بَعْدَ كَوْنِهِ مَجَازاً مُشْتَرِكاً فَلَا يَعُمُّ، أَمَّا عِنْدَنَا فَلِأَنَّ الْمُشْتَرَكَ لَا عُمُومَ لَهُ وَإِذَا ثَبَتَ الْأُخْرَوِيُّ إِجْمَاعاً يَثْبُتُ الْآخَرُ كَذَا فِي التَّنْقِيحِ (٣٥) وَتَمَامُهُ فِي شَرْحِنَا عَلَى الْمَنَارِ وَأَمَّا الْحُكْمُ الدُّنْيَوِيُّ فَإِنْ وَقَعَ فِي تَرْكِ مَأْمُورٍ لَمْ يَسْقُطْ بَلْ يَجِبُ تَدَارُكُهُ وَلَا يَحْصُلُ الثَّوَابُ الْمُتَرَتِّبُ عَلَيْهِ وَلَوْ عَلَى فِعْلِ مَنْهِيٍّ عَنْهُ فَإِنَّهُ أَوْجَبَ عُقُوبَةً كَانَ شُبْهَةً فِي إِسْقَاطِهَا فَمَنْ نَسِيَ صَلَاةً أَوْ صَوْماً أَوْ حَجّاً أَوْ زَكَاةً أَوْ كَفَّارَةً أَوْ نَذْراً وَجَبَ قَضَاؤُهُ بِلَا خِلَافٍ وَكَذَا لَوْ وَقَفَ بِغَيْرِ عَرَفَةَ غَلَطاً يَجِبُ الْقَضَاءُ اتِّفَاقاً

---

٣٣) انظر / الأشباه والنظائر للسيوطى ٢٠٦ / طه عيسى الحلى.

٣٤) أخرجه ابن ماجه برقم ٢٠٤٥ عن ابن عباس في كتاب الطلاق ١/ ٦٥٩ وأبو نعيم بحلية الأولياء ٣٥٢/٦ عن ابن عباس / ط - السعادة.

٣٥) انظر / التلويح على التوضيح ٢ / ١٦٩. ط - صبيح.

> explanation of *al-Manār*. As for the worldly ruling, if the forgetfulness happens with regard to leaving an ordered act, then the obligation does not drop. Rather, it is to be made up, despite him not obtaining the reward stipulated for it. The reward expected from it is not attained, even if it was a prohibited act for which a punishment was presumed, as the doubt in its annulment is dispelled. Hence, whoever forgets a prayer, fasting, pilgrimage, alms, expiation, or vow must make it up without disagreement.

Similarly, if someone stood at a place other than ʿArafāt during Hajj unintentionally, they must make it up, which is an agreed upon conclusion. Also, if someone unknowingly prayed with an impermissible amount of impurity on them, or forgot a pillar of prayer, or became certain that they were mistaken in determining the validity of water, clothing, time for prayer and fasting, or the intention for fasting, or spoke during prayer forgetfully, their act of worship remains valid. Among the matters whose ruling is dropped due to forgetfulness is that if someone eats or drinks forgetfully while fasting, it does not nullify the fast, unlike if they intentionally ate or drank. Likewise, if someone gives the *salām* mistakenly during the two-unit prayer, it does not nullify it, whether intentionally or unintentionally, contrary to omitting the pronouncement during slaughter."

Another issue related to forgetfulness is found when a debtor forgets a debt and then dies. If the debt was a sale price or a loan, it is not taken from his estate, but if it was acquired forcibly, then it is collected. That is how it is mentioned in criminal cases. Additionally, if a testator knows that the person he is bequeathing to has left a will but forgets its amount, then the ruling is discussed in *Waṣāyā Khizānah al-Muftīn*.

وَمِنْهَا مَنْ صَلَّى بِنَجَاسَةٍ مَانِعَةٍ نَاسِياً أَوْ نَسِيَ رُكْناً مِنْ أَرْكَانِ الصَّلَاةِ أَوْ تَيَقَّنَ الْخَطَأَ فِي الْاِجْتِهَادِ فِي الْمَاءِ وَالثَّوْبِ وَوَقْتِ الصَّلَاةِ وَالصَّوْمِ أَوْ نَسِيَ نِيَّةَ الصَّوْمِ أَوْ تَكَلَّمَ فِي الصَّلَاةِ نَاسِياً وَمِمَّا سَقَطَ حُكْمُهُ فِي النِّسْيَانِ لَوْ أَكَلَ أَوْ شَرِبَ نَاسِياً فِي الصَّوْمِ أَوْ جَامَعَ لَمْ يَبْطُلْ أَوْ أَكَلَ نَاسِياً فِي الصَّلَاةِ تَبْطُلُ لَا لَوْ سَلَّمَ نَاسِياً فِي الصَّلَاةِ الرُّبَاعِيَّةِ عَلَى رَأْسِ رَكْعَتَيْنِ وَالنَّاسِي وَالْعَامِدُ بِالْيَمِينِ سَوَاءٌ، وَكَذَا فِي الطَّلَاقِ لَوْ قَالَ زَوْجَتِي طَالِقٌ نَاسِياً أَنَّ لَهُ زَوْجَةً وَكَذَا فِي الْعِتَاقِ وَكَذَا فِي مَحْظُورَاتِ الْإِحْرَامِ وَلَقَدْ جُعِلَ لَهُ أَصْلٌ فِي التَّحْرِيرِ وَقَالَ: إِنَّهُ إِنْ كَانَ مَعَ تَذَكُّرٍ وَلَا أَدْعَى لَهُ كَأَكْلِ الْمُصَلِّي لَمْ يَسْقُطْ لِتَقْصِيرِهِ بِخِلَافِ سَلَامِهِ فِي الْقَعْدَةِ الْأُولَى أَوَّلَا مَعَهُ مَعَ دَاعِي كَأَكْلِ الصَّائِمِ سَقَطَ أَوَّلَا وَإِلَّا فَالْأَوْلَى كَتَرْكِ الذَّابِحِ التَّسْمِيَةَ. اِنْتَهَى.

وَمِنْ مَسَائِلِ النِّسْيَانِ لَوْ نَسِيَ الْمَدْيُونُ الدَّيْنَ وَمَاتَ فَإِنْ كَانَ ثَمَنَ مَبِيعٍ أَوْ قَرْضٍ لَمْ يُؤْخَذْ بِهِ وَإِنْ كَانَ غَصْباً يُؤَاخَذُ بِهِ كَذَا فِي الْجِنَايَةِ وَمِنْهَا لَوْ عَلِمَ الْوَصِيُّ بِأَنَّ الْمُوصِي أَوْصَى بِوِصَايَةٍ لَكِنَّهُ نَسِيَ مِقْدَارَهَا وَحُكْمُهُ فِي (وَصَايَا خِزَانَةِ الْمُفْتِينَ).

Epilogue

This is an elucidation that forgetfulness does not detract from the perfection of human beings and that it is permissible for Prophets. However, it only occurred to them in matters unrelated to what they were obligated to convey. Allah, may He be exalted, said: "And We had already taken a promise from Adam before, but he forgot; and We found not in him determination."[49]

Al-Bayḍāwī said:

> "[It means] 'and We commanded him'. It is said that an Angel came to him and exhorted him...and he adjured him and took a covenant from him regarding what he had commanded him. The *lām* (in the original Arabic) is the predicate of an omitted oath. The story of Adam was only juxtaposed to His words 'And We exhibited therein divine threats' is an indication that the Children of Ādam are prone to forgetfulness and that forgetfulness is firmly rooted in them. 'Before' means before this time. 'But he forgot' the covenant and did not concern himself with it. An alternative interpretation is that he left what he was commanded to do, namely avoiding the tree. 'But We found not in him determination': determination (*ʿazm*) means the firm resolution and perseverance upon the command. That is because if he was resolute and firm, Shayṭān would not have made him slip, nor would he have been able to deceive him. And perhaps that was before the beginning of his affair, and before he had tried the affairs and tasted their sweetness and sourness."

The Imam, Muḥaddith, ʿAllāmah, and exemplary scholar Najm al-Dīn al-Ghazzī ﷺ mentioned in his book *Ḥusn al-Tanbīh fī Mā Warada fī al-Tashbīh* that one of the characteristics of the accursed Satan is to make the servant forget to remember his Lord during his times of distress and need. This is so that the servant feels inclined to seek help and succour from others due to their status, word, or power.

49 *Ṭā Hā*, 115.

الخَاتِمَةُ

فِي بَيَانِ أَنَّ النِّسيَانَ لَيسَ بِنُقْصَانٍ فِي كَمَالِ الْإِنْسَانِ وَأَنَّهُ يَجُوزُ عَلَى الْأَنْبِيَاءِ وَوَقَعَ مِنْهُمْ فِي غَيْرِ مَا وَجَبَ عَلَيْهِ تَبْلِيغُهُ مِنَ الْأَحْكَامِ وَوُرُودُ الْآيَاتِ فِي ذَلِكَ وَالْأَخْبَارِ قَالَ اللهُ تَعَالَى[٣٦] ﴿وَلَقَدْ عَهِدْنَا إِلَىٰ آدَمَ مِن قَبْلُ فَنَسِيَ وَلَمْ نَجِدْ لَهُ عَزْمًا﴾ قَالَ الْبَيْضَاوِيُّ ﴿وَلَقَدْ عَهِدْنَا إِلَىٰ آدَمَ﴾ وَلَقَدْ أَمَرْنَاهُ يُقَالُ: تَقَدَّمَ المُلْكُ إليهِ، وَأَوْعَزَ إِلَيهِ وعَزَمَ عَلَيهِ وَعَهِدَ إِلَيهِ إِذَا أَمَرَهُ، وَاللَّامُ جَوَابُ قَسَمٍ مَحْذُوفٍ، وَإِنَّمَا عَطَفَ قِصَّةَ آدَمَ عَلَى قَوْلِهِ: ﴿وَصَرَّفْنا فِيهِ مِنَ الوَعِيدِ﴾. لِلدَّلَالَةِ على أَنَّ أَساسَ بَنِي آدمَ عَلَى العِصْيَانِ، وعِرْقُهُمْ راسِخٌ فِي النِّسيانِ. ﴿مِنْ قَبْلُ﴾ مِنْ قِبَلِ هٰذا الزَّمانِ. ﴿فَنَسِيَ﴾ العَهْدَ، وَلَمْ يعِنْ بِهِ حتَّىٰ غَفَلَ عَنْهُ، أَوْ تَرَكَ مَا وُصِيَ بِهِ مِنَ الاِحْتِرازِ عنِ الشَّجَرَةِ. ﴿وَلَمْ نَجِدْ لَهُ عَزْماً﴾ تَصْمِيمَ رَأْيٍ وَثَباتاً عَلَى الْأَمْرِ؛ إِذْ لَوْ كَانَ ذا عَزِيمَةٍ وَتَصَلُّبٍ لَمْ يَزِلَّهُ الشَّيْطَانُ وَلَمْ يَسْتَطِعْ تَغْرِيرَهُ، وَلَعَلَّ ذٰلِكَ كانَ فِي بَدْءِ أَمْرِهِ قَبْلَ أَنْ يُجَرِّبَ الأُمُورَ وَيَذُوقَ شَرِيهَا وَأَرِيها. وَذَكَرَ الْإِمَامُ الْمُحَدِّثُ الْعَلَّامَةُ الْعُمْدَةُ نَجْمُ الدِّينِ الْغَزِّيّ رَحِمَهُ اللهُ تَعَالَى فِي كِتَابِ حُسْنِ التَّنْبِيهِ فِي مَا وَرَدَ فِي التَّشْبِيهِ قَالَ: وَمِنْ أَخْلَاقِ الشَّيْطَانِ اللَّعِينِ إِنْسَاءُ الْعَبْدِ أَنْ يَذْكُرَ رَبَّهُ فِي شَدَائِدِهِ وَحَاجَاتِهِ، فَيُلْقِي فِي قَلْبِ الْعَبْدِ طَلَبَ الْغَوْثِ وَالْحَاجَةِ مِنَ الْعَبْدِ لِمَا لَهُ مِنْ جَاهٍ أَوْ كَلِمَةٍ أَوْ قُوَّةٍ، فَمَنْ اِسْتَشَارَكَ فِي مُهِمَّةٍ أَوْ مَلَمَّةٍ فَأَرْشِدْهُ أَوَّلًا إِلَى أَنْ يَرْفَعَ حَاجَتَهُ إِلَى اللهِ

---

٣٦) سورة طه الآية ١١٥.

Therefore, whoever seeks your advice regarding an important matter or a crisis, firstly advise them to advance their need to Allah, rely on Him, and await goodness from Him. Then, advise them based on what you see appropriate. Beware of directing them to seek assistance from a so-called fortune-teller or a sinful person, as this would align you with the brothers of the devils.

Allah ﷻ said, quoting Yūsuf ﷺ, "He said to the one of the two who he believed would be saved,"[50] meaning the one that would serve wine to the king. He was one of the two youths that sought guidance from him regarding what they saw in their dream: "Mention me in the presence of your Lord. But Shayṭān caused him to forget to remember his lord. So, he remained in prison for some years."[51]

Al-Baghawī stated:

> "Ibn ʿAbbās ﷺ said, and it is the assertion of most [of the scholars of *tafsīr*], 'The Shayṭān caused Yūsuf to forget the remembrance of his Lord until he sought relief from other than Him and sought help in a created being. And that was a slip that Yūsuf committed through the influence Shayṭān.' Al-Qurṭubī said: 'However, some scholars considered this problematic because Shayṭān has no authority over the Prophets. So how could the forgetfulness of Yūsuf be attributed to him? The answer for this is that the Prophets ﷺ are not protected from forgetfulness, except in that which they are to convey from Allah ﷻ. As for other things, when forgetfulness occurs from them, whereas its occurrence from them is possible, it is attributed to Shayṭān without exception. And it is only attributed to them in that with which Allah has informed us about them. In other words, it is not permissible for us to attribute it to them.'
>
> An example of this is in the statement of Yūshaʿ, 'And only the Shayṭān caused me to forget to mention it'.[52] Thus the remembrance of the fish was attributed to Mūsā ﷺ.

50 *Yūsuf*, 42.

51 *Yūsuf*, 42.

52 *al-Kahf*, 63.

تَعَالَى وَاعْتِمَادَهُ عَلَيْهِ وَانْتِظَارَ الْخَيْرِ مِنْهُ ثُمَّ أَشِرْ عَلَيْهِ بِمَا تَرَى وَإِيَّاكَ أَنْ تُشِيرَ إِلَيْهِ أَنْ يَلْجَأَ إِلَى مُتَوَجِّهٍ أَوْ فَاسِقٍ فَتَكُونَ مِنْ إِخْوَانِ الشَّيَاطِينِ. قَالَ اللهُ تَعَالَى حِكَايَةً عَنْ يُوسُفَ عَلَيْهِ السَّلَامُ [37] ﴿وَقَالَ لِلَّذِي ظَنَّ أَنَّهُ نَاجٍ مِّنْهُمَا﴾ يَعْنِي السَّاقِيَ الْمَلِكِ، وَهُوَ أَحَدُ الْفَتَيَيْنِ اللَّذَيْنِ اسْتَفْتَيَاهُ فِيمَا رَآهُ فِي مَنَامِهِ ﴿اذْكُرْنِي عِندَ رَبِّكَ فَأَنسَاهُ الشَّيْطَانُ ذِكْرَ رَبِّهِ فَلَبِثَ فِي السِّجْنِ بِضْعَ سِنِينَ﴾ [38] قَالَ البغوي: قال ابن عباس رضي الله عنه وعليه أكثرون: أَنْسَى الشَّيْطَانُ يُوسُفَ ذِكْرَ رَبِّهِ حَتَّى ابْتَغَى الْفَرَجَ مِنْ غَيْرِهِ، وَاسْتَعَانَ بِمَخْلُوقٍ، وَتِلْكَ غَفْلَةٌ عَرَضَتْ لِيُوسُفَ مِنَ الشَّيْطَانِ. وَاسْتَشْكَلَ هَذَا بَعْضُهُمْ، لِأَنَّ الشَّيْطَانَ لَيْسَ لَهُ عَلَى الْأَنْبِيَاءِ سُلْطَةٌ فَكَيْفَ يُضَافُ نِسْيَانُ يُوسُفَ إِلَى الشَّيْطَانِ، وَأُجِيبُ بِأَنَّ الْأَنْبِيَاءَ عَلَيْهِمُ الصَّلَاةُ وَالسَّلَامُ لَا عِصْمَةَ لَهُمْ مِنَ النِّسْيَانِ إِلَّا فِيمَا يُبَلِّغُونَ عَنِ اللهِ تَعَالَى فَقَطْ، وَأَمَّا فِي غَيْرِهِ فَإِذَا وَقَعَ النِّسْيَانُ مِنْهُمْ حَيْثُ يُحْذَرُ وُقُوعُهُ فَإِنَّهُ يُنْسَبُ إِلَى الشَّيْطَانِ إِطْلَاقاً، وَذَلِكَ فِيمَا يُخْبِرُ اللهُ عَنْهُمْ، وَلَا يَجُوزُ لَنَا نَحْنُ ذَلِكَ. قَالَ الْقُرْطُبِيُّ: وَنَظِيرُ ذَلِكَ قَوْلُ يُوشَعَ بْنِ نُونٍ ﴿وَمَا أَنسَانِيهُ إِلَّا الشَّيْطَانُ أَنْ أَذْكُرَهُ﴾ [39] فَنَسَبَ ذِكْرَ الْحُوتِ إِلَى مُوسَى عَلَيْهِ السَّلَامُ، وَالتَّحْقِيقُ فِي هَذِهِ الْمَسْأَلَةِ أَنَّ تَسْلِيطَ الشَّيْطَانِ عَلَى الْأَنْبِيَاءِ

---

٣٧) سورة يوسف الآية ٤٢.

٣٨) سورة يوسف الآية ٤٢.

٣٩) سورة الكهف الآية ٦٣.

The confirmed verdict on this issue is that Shayṭān's influence on the Prophets ﷺ regarding matters that affect their disposition or bodies – without diverting them from steadfastness under the burdens of prophecy and conveying the message as they were commanded – does not diminish their rank; they turn to Allah in the end. Rather, this is only an intensification of their test because they are the most severely tested of people. This is similar to how Shayṭān affected Adam ﷺ until he tasted the tree, despite Adam's keenness not to disobey his Lord's command. It is also similar to how it affected Yaʿqūb ﷺ until he was tested with that beyond which he could not bear.

Likewise, magic affected the body of the Messenger of Allah ﷺ.[53]

ʿAbdullāh Ibn Muhammad narrated to me, saying: I heard Ibn ʿUyaynah say: Ibn Jurayj narrated to us, saying: Āl ʿUrwah narrated to me on the authority of ʿUrwah: I asked Hishām about it and he narrated to us from his father that ʿĀ'ishah ﷺ said, 'The Messenger of Allah ﷺ was affected by magic to the point that he thought that he had been with his women when he actually had not.' Sufyān said, 'And that is the most intense form of magic when it affects one in such a way.' He (the Messenger of Allah ﷺ) said, 'O ʿĀ'ishah, did you know that Allah has given me a solution to that for which I sought a solution from Him? Two men came to me. One of them sat at my head. The other sat at my feet. The one who sat at my head said to the other, "What is the matter with this man?" The latter replied, "He has had magic done on him." The first said, "Who has done magic on him?" The latter replied, "Labīd ibn al-Aʿṣam, a man from the Banū Zurayq, an ally of the Jews and a hypocrite." The first asked, "What has he used?" He said, "[He has done it] on a comb and a hair stuck to it." The first asked, "Where is it?" The latter replied, "In the pollen skin of a male date palm, hidden under a stone in the well of Dharwān." So, the Prophet ﷺ went to the well and took it out. He said, "This is the well that I was shown. It is as if its water has been infused with henna and its datepalms are like the heads of

53 It was narrated by al-Bukhārī, Hadith no. 5765.

فِيمَا يُؤَثِّرُ فِي طِبَاعِهِمْ أَوْ فِي أَجْسَادِهِمْ مِنْ غَيْرِ أَنْ يُزَحْزِحَهُمْ عَنِ الثَّبَاتِ تَحْتَ أَعْبَاءِ النُّبُوَّةِ وَعَنِ التَّبْلِيغِ كَمَا أُمِرُوا لَا يَقْدَحُ فِي رُتْبَتِهِمْ لِأَنَّهُمْ يَفِيئُونَ إِلَى اللهِ تَعَالَى فِي آخِرِ أَمْرِهِمْ، وَإِنَّمَا يَكُونُ ذَلِكَ لِمَزِيدٍ مِنَ الْإِبْتِلَاءِ لِأَنَّهُمْ أَشَدُّ النَّاسِ بَلَاءً، وَذَلِكَ كَمَا أَثَّرَ كَلَامُ الشَّيْطَانِ فِي نَفْسِ آدَمَ عَلَيْهِ السَّلَامُ حَتَّى ذَاقَ الشَّجَرَةَ، وَقَدْ كَانَ شَدِيدَ الْحِرْصِ عَلَى أَلَّا يُخَالِفَ أَمْرَ رَبِّهِ، وَكَمَا أَثَّرَ فِي بَدَنِ يَعْقُوبَ عَلَيْهِ السَّلَامُ حَتَّى اِبْتُلِيَ بِمَا لَا مَزِيدَ عَلَيْهِ، وَكَمَا أَثَّرَ السِّحْرُ فِي بَدَنِ رَسُولِ اللهِ ﷺ [٤٠] حدَّثني عبدُ اللهِ بنُ محمدٍ قال: سمعتُ ابنَ عُيينةَ يَقُولُ: حَدَّثَنَا بِهِ ابْنُ جُرَيْجٍ يَقُولُ: حَدَّثَنِي آلُ عُرْوَةٍ عَنْ عُرْوَةَ فَسَأَلْتُ هِشَامَ عَنْهُ فَحَدَّثَنَا عَنْ أَبِيهِ عَنْ عَائِشَةَ رَضِيَ اللهُ عَنْهَا قَالَ: كَانَ رَسُولُ اللهِ ﷺ سُحِرَ حَتَّى كَانَ يَرَى أَنَّهُ يَأْتِي النِّسَاءَ وَلَا يَأْتِيهِنَّ؛ قَالَ سُفْيَانُ: وَهَذَا أَشَدُّ مَا يَكُونُ مِنَ السِّحْرِ إِذَا كَانَ كَذَا، فَقَالَ: يَا عَائِشَةُ: اَعَلِمْتِ أَنَّ اللهَ أَفْتَانِي فِيمَا اِسْتَفْتَيْتُهُ فِيهِ؟ آتَانِي رَجُلَانِ فَقَعَدَ أَحَدُهُمَا عِنْدَ رَأْسِي وَالْآخَرُ عِنْدَ رِجْلَيَّ، فَقَالَ الَّذِي عِنْدَ رَأْسِي لِلْآخَرِ: مَا بَالُ الرَّجُلِ؟ فَقَالَ: مَطْبُوبٌ. قَالَ مَنْ طَبَّهُ؟ قَالَ لَبِيدُ بْنُ الْأَعْصَمِ رَجُل مِنْ بَنِي زُرَيْقٍ حَلِيفٌ لِلْيَهُودِ كَانَ مُنَافِقاً قَالَ وَفِيمَ؟ قَالَ فِي مِشْطٍ وَمُشَاطَةٍ. قَالَ: وَأَيْنَ؟ قَالَ: فِي جُفِّ طَلْعَةٍ ذَكَرٍ، تَحْتَ رَعُوفَةٍ فِي بِئْرِ ذَرْوَانَ قَالَتْ: فَأَتَى النَّبِيُّ ﷺ الْبِئْرَ حَتَّى اِسْتَخْرَجَهُ فَقَالَ هَذِهِ الْبِئْرُ الَّتِي أُرِيتُهَا وَكَأَنَّ مَاءَهَا نَقَاعَةُ الْحِنَّاءِ وَكَأَنَّ نَخْلَهَا رُؤُوسُ الشَّيَاطِينِ قَالَ فَاسْتُخْرِجَ.

---

٤٠) أخرجه البخاري في صحيحه ٨ / ٢٢ عن عائشة / ط. دار الجيل وابن ماجة ٢ / ١١٧٣.

> devils." So, he took it out.
>
> [ʿĀ'ishah said,] 'I said, "Will you not seek reprisals?" The Prophet ﷺ responded, "Indeed, by Allah, Allah has cured me. And I hate to inflict evil upon anyone among mankind."'
>
> In another narration, it caused him ﷺ to think that he had done something while he had not really done it, or that he had gone to his women while he had not gone to them. This state continued until Allah sent the Angel who cured him with the Muʿawwidhatayn.[54]
>
> The situation of Yūsuf ﷺ – when Shayṭān caused him to forget to remember his Lord – is also from this kind of occurrence."

Forgetfulness has also occurred to our Prophet Muhammad ﷺ, as was narrated by al-Bukhārī from Aḥmad ibn Abī Rajā', who said: Abū Usāmah narrated to us from Hishām ibn ʿUrwah from his father that ʿĀ'ishah said, "The Messenger of Allah ﷺ heard a man reciting a *sūrah* during the night. He said, 'May Allah have mercy on him. He has reminded us of such and such verse which we had forgotten in such and such *sūrah*.'"[55]

And the Prophet Muhammad ﷺ used to lead the people in prayer, and he once skipped a verse of the Qur'an while reciting in prayer, and then he asked if Ubayy ibn Kaʿb was present among the congregation.[56]

And Allah ﷻ addressed our Prophet Muhammad ﷺ saying: "We will make you recite, and you will not forget except what Allah wills. Indeed, He knows what is declared openly and what is hidden."[57]

Al-Bayḍāwī said:

> "'We will make you recite' upon the tongue of Jibrīl. Alternatively, it means that We will make you a reciter by inspiring recitation to you. 'And you will not forget' at all from the strength of your

54 Sūrahs al-Falaq and al-Nās.

55 *al-Sunan al-Kubrā li al-Bayhaqī*, vol. 3, p. 12.

56 *Musnad Imām Aḥmad*, vol. 3, p. 407.

57 *al-Aʿlā*, 6-7.

قَالَتْ فَقُلْتُ: أَفَلَا - أَيْ تَنَشَّرْتَ-؟ فَقَالَ أَمَا وَاللهِ فَقَدْ شَفَانِي اللهُ وَأَكْرَهُ أَنْ أُثِيرَ عَلَى أَحَدٍ مِنَ النَّاسِ شَرّاً. أَوْ وَفِي فِكْرِهِ حَتَّى كَانَ يُخَيَّلُ إِلَيْهِ أَنَّهُ فَعَلَ الشَّيْءَ وَمَا فَعَلَهُ وَأَنَّهُ أَتَى النِّسَاءَ وَمَا آتَاهُنَّ حَتَّى بَعَثَ اللهُ تَعَالَى إِلَيْهِ الْمَلَكَ فَرَقَاهُ الْمُعَوِّذَتَيْنِ. وَكَانَ حَالُ يُوسُفَ عَلَيْهِ السَّلَامُ حِينَ أَنْسَاهُ الشَّيْطَانُ ذِكْرَ رَبِّهِ مِنْ هَذَا الْقَبِيلِ اِنْتَهَى كَلَامُهُ وَقَدْ وَقَعَ النِّسْيَانُ لِنَبِيِّنَا مُحَمَّدٍ ﷺ كَمَا أَخْرَجَهُ الْبُخَارِيُّ عَنْ أَحْمَدَ بْنِ أَبِي رَجَا. قَالَ حَدَّثَنَا أَبُو أُسَامَةَ عَنْ هِشَامِ بْنِ عُرْوَةَ عَنْ أَبِيهِ عَنْ عَائِشَةَ [٤١] قَالَ سَمِعَ رَسُولُ اللهِ ﷺ رَجُلاً يَقْرَأُ فِي سُورَةٍ بِاللَّيْلِ فَقَالَ يَرْحَمُهُ اللهُ لَقَدْ أَذْكَرَنِي كَذَا وَكَذَا آيَةً كُنْتُ نَسِيتُهَا مِنْ سُورَةِ كَذَا وَكَذَا وَكَانَ النَّبِيُّ ﷺ يَؤُمُّ النَّاسَ فِي الصَّلَاةِ فَأَسْقَطَ آيَةً مِنَ الْقُرْآنِ فِي التِّلَاوَةِ فَقَالَ أَفِي الْقَوْمِ أُبَيٌّ [٤٢] وَقَالَ اللهُ تَعَالَى خِطَاباً لِنَبِيِّنَا مُحَمَّدٍ ﷺ [٤٣] ﴿سَنُقْرِئُكَ فَلَا تَنسَىٰ ۝ إِلَّا مَا شَاءَ اللَّهُ إِنَّهُ يَعْلَمُ الْجَهْرَ وَمَا يَخْفَىٰ ۝﴾ قَالَ الْبَيْضَاوِيُّ: سَنُقْرِئُكَ عَلَى لِسَانِ جِبْرِيلَ أَوْ سَنَجْعَلُكَ قَارِئاً بِإِلْهَامِ الْقِرَاءَةِ، وُقُوعُهُ كَذَلِكَ أَيْضاً مِنَ الْآيَاتِ، وَقِيلَ نَهْيٌ وَالْأَلِفُ لِلْفَاصِلَةِ كَقَوْلِهِ إِلَّا مَا شَاءَ اللهُ نِسْيَانَهُ بِأَنْ نَسَخَ

---

٤١) أخرجه البيهقي في السنن الكبرى ٣ / ١٢ ط الهند، والبخاري عن عائشة ٦ / ٢٣٨ دار الجيل

٤٢) أخرجه أحمد عن ابن ابزى ٣ / ٤٠٧.

٤٣) سورة الأعلى آية ٦.

> memory, despite the fact that you are unlettered, so that will be another sign in your support. This is despite the fact that his being informed about things that would happen in the future, and their occurring, was also among his signs. It has also been said that this was an order and that the *alif* (*maqṣūrah*) is an extra letter, just like when He said *al-sabīlā*.[58] 'Except what Allah wills' from it being forgotten, that is, by abrogating its recitation. It has also been said that He meant by that a small amount and rarely, due to what has been narrated, namely that he ﷺ left out a verse in his recitation during the prayer. So, Ubayy believed that it had been abrogated. But when he asked him, the Prophet ﷺ replied, 'I forgot it.' It has also been said that it negates any forgetting at all, because 'a little' has been used for absolute negation. 'Indeed, He knows what is open and what is hidden' means your apparent and hidden states. Or it refers to reciting the Qur'an loudly with Jibrīl ﷺ and what causes you to do so of your fear of forgetting. And He knows where – in retention or forgetfulness – lies your benefit."

The author – may Allah benefit us by him – said, "This is the last of what we intended to include in this letter, relying on Allah for assistance. We ask Him, glorified be He, to disseminate its benefit and to aid the brothers in preserving the integrated sciences towards achieving contentment and enjoying the noble position. The composition of this message was done in two sessions, the last of which was on Thursday, the second of the month of Rabīᶜ al-Awwal, in the year 1106 AH. May Allah send prayers upon our master Muhammad, his Family, and Companions, and grant them peace until the Day of Judgment."

---

58 *al-Aḥzāb*, 67.

تِلَاوَتَهُ، وَقِيلَ الْمُرَادُ بِهِ الْقِلَّةُ وَالنُّدْرَةُ لِمَا رُوِيَ أَنَّهُ عَلَيْهِ السَّلَامُ أَسْقَطَ آيَةً مِنْ قِرَاءَتِهِ فِي الصَّلَاةِ فَحَسِبَ أُبَيٌّ رَضِيَ اللهُ عَنْهُ أَنَّهَا نُسِخَتْ فَسَأَلَهُ فَقَالَ نَسِيتُهَا، أَوْ نَفْيُ النِّسْيَانِ رَأْساً فَإِنَّ الْقِلَّةَ تُسْتَعْمَلُ لِلنَّفْيِ، إِنَّهُ يَعْلَمُ الْجَهْرَ وَمَا يَخْفَى: مَا ظَهَرَ مِنْ أَحْوَالِكُمْ وَمَا بَطَنَ أَوْ جَهْرَكَ بِالْقِرَاءَةِ مَعَ جِبْرِيلَ وَمَا دَعَاكَ إِلَيْهِ مِنْ مُخَالَفَةِ النِّسْيَانِ فَيَعْلَمُ مَا فِيهِ صَلَاحُكُمْ مِنْ إِبْقَاءٍ أَوْ إِنْسَاءٍ اِنْتَهَى.

قَالَ الْمُؤَلِّفُ نَفَعَنَا اللهُ تَعَالَى بِهِ وَهَذَا آخِرُ مَا قَصَدْنَا إِيرَادَهُ فِي هَذِهِ الرِّسَالَةِ بِحَسَبِ الْإِمْكَانِ وَبِاللهِ الْمُسْتَعَانُ وَنَسْأَلُهُ سُبْحَانَهُ أَنْ يُدِيمَ بِهَا الْإِفَادَةَ وَيُعِينَ الْإِخْوَانَ عَلَى حِفْظِ الْعُلُومِ الْمُوصِلَةِ إِلَى حُصُولِ السَّعَادَةِ وَالتَّمَتُّعِ بِمَقَامِ الْحُسْنَى وَزِيَادَةِ وَكَانَ التَّأْلِيفُ لِهَذِهِ الرِّسَالَةِ فِي مَجْلِسَيْنِ آخِرُهُمَا يَوْمُ الْخَمِيسِ الثَّانِي مِنْ شَهْرِ رَبِيعِ الْأَوَّلِ سَنَةَ سِتٍّ وَمِائَةٍ وَأَلْفٍ وَصَلَّى اللهُ عَلَى سَيِّدِنَا مُحَمَّدٍ وَعَلَى آلِهِ وَصَحْبِهِ وَسَلَّمَ تَسْلِيماً إِلَى يَوْمِ الدِّينِ.

Book Two

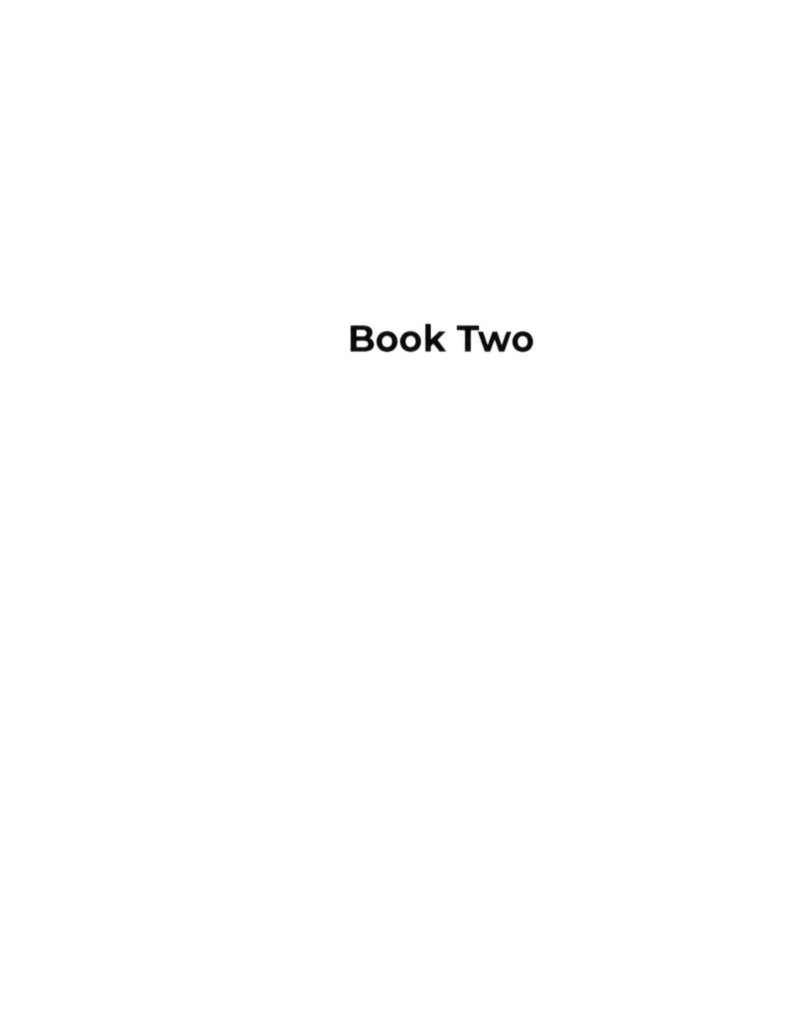

الكِتَابُ الثَانِي

THE CURE FOR FORGETFULNESS

COMPILED BY

ḤABĪB MUHAMMAD IBN ʿALAWĪ AL-ʿAYDARŪS

IMAM OF MASJID AL-SAQQĀF IN TARĪM

عِلَاجُ النِّسْيَانِ

جَمْعُ السَّيِّدِ مُحَمَّدُ بْنُ عَلَوِي الْعَيْدَرُوسِ
إِمَامُ مَسْجِدِ السَّقَّافِ بِتريم

In the Name of Allah, the Most Beneficent, the Most Merciful

Introduction

Many individuals in our age complain of the difficulty of memorizing or forgetting that which they had memorized while they were children or in adulthood. That deficiency can be traced to the prevalent anxiety and tension that has dominated people's lives in this strange time, in which falsehood reigns and corruption has spread throughout the lands and among the servants of the divine. All of this has caused, among the Muslims, an acute lack of quietude and tranquillity. This is especially so with the wars of starvation and manufactured economic crises that distract the Muslim from worshipping his Lord and cause him to become distant from the Qur'an. There is no doubt that this is a chief driver of this problem. However, the strength of the truth is superior to every complication or malady. Our strength lies in the gift of thought, remembrance, steadfastness with the Qur'an, and having beneficial knowledge in our hearts and minds, by the permission of Allah. "And I have never been, my Lord, in supplicating You, disappointed."[1] The Qur'an has a glimmering light which can never be concealed. It also has its faithful people who memorize it from generation to generation: "Indeed, We are revealing the remembrance. And indeed, We are preserving it."[2] What highlights the love of people for the Qur'an is their efforts to listen to it day and night, and their sincere hope for themselves and their descendants to memorize the Qur'an. It is for that reason that I put forth for you, my honoured lover of the Book of Allah who desires to memorize it, some verses and supplications which the scholars, righteous folk, and seekers of knowledge have tried and tested towards this end, which will help one to quickly memorize and retain what is read. In our view, they prevent episodes of forgetfulness, even if only for a portion of that which one has memorized.

---

1 *Maryam*, 4.

2 *al-Ḥijr*, 9.

بِسْمِ اللهِ الرَّحْمَنِ الرَّحِيمِ

الْمُقَدِّمَةُ

كَثِيرٌ مِنَ النَّاسِ فِي زَمَانِنَا يَشْكُونَ مِنْ صُعُوبَةِ الْحِفْظِ وَنِسْيَانِ مَا كَانَ مَحْفُوظاً لَدَيْهِمْ مُنْذُ الصِّغَرِ أَوِ الْكِبَرِ وَذَلِكَ لِلْقَلَقِ وَالتَّوَتُّرِ الْمُسَيْطِرِ عَلَى دُنْيَا النَّاسِ فِي هَذَا الزَّمَانِ الْعَجِيبِ الَّذِي حَكَمَ فِيهِ الْبَاطِلُ وَسَادَ الْفَسَادُ فِي الْبِلَادِ وَالْعِبَادِ مِمَّا يُحْدِثُ فِي الْمُسْلِمِ عَدَمَ الْأَمَانِ وَعَدَمَ الْإِسْتِقْرَارِ، خُصُوصاً مَعَ حَرْبِ التَّجْوِيعِ وَاصْطِنَاعِ الْمَشَاكِلِ الْاِقْتِصَادِيَّةِ لِشُغْلِ الْمُسْلِمِ عَنْ عِبَادَةِ رَبِّهِ وَهَجْرِ كِتَابِ اللهِ، وَلاَ شَكَّ أَنَّ لِذَلِكَ تَأْثِيرٌ كَبِيرٌ وَلَكِنَّ قُوَّةَ الْحَقِّ فَوْقَ الْجَمِيعِ، وَعَظَمَةٌ عَلَيْنَا مَوْهِبَةُ الْفِكْرِ وَالذِّكْرِ وَثَبَاتُ كِتَابِ اللهِ وَالْعِلْمِ النَّافِعِ فِي قُلُوبِنَا وَعُقُولِنَا بِإِذْنِ اللهِ ﴿وَلَمْ أَكُن بِدُعَائِكَ رَبِّ شَقِيًّا﴾ [مَرْيَمُ: ٤].

الْقُرْآنُ لَهُ نُورٌ لَا يَخْبَأُ أَبداً وَلَهُ رِجَالُهُ وَحَفَظَتُهُ ﴿إِنَّا نَحْنُ نَزَّلْنَا الذِّكْرَ وَإِنَّا لَهُ لَحَافِظُونَ﴾ [الْحِجْرُ: ٩].

وَمِمَّا يُؤَكِّدُ حُبَّ النَّاسِ لِلْقُرْآنِ الْكَرِيمِ سَعْيُهُمْ لَيْلاً وَنَهَاراً لِسَمَاعِهِ وَتَمَنِّيهِمْ أَنْ يَحْفَظُوهُ وَأَنْ تَكُونَ ذُرِّيَتُهُمْ مِنْ حَفَظَةِ كِتَابِ اللَّهِ.

مِنْ أَجْلِ ذَلِكَ أُقَدِّمُ لَكَ عَزِيزِي الْمُحِبُّ لِكِتَابِ اللَّهِ وَحِفْظِهِ آيَاتٍ وَدَعَوَاتٍ جَرَّبَهَا الْعُلَمَاءُ وَالصَّالِحُونَ وَطُلَّابُ الْعِلْمِ، فَهِيَ تُسَاعِدُ عَلَى سُرْعَةِ الْحِفْظِ وَتَقْضِي عَلَى دَائِرَةِ النِّسْيَانِ، وَلَوْ جُزْءٌ مِنْهَا عِنْدَنَا بِمَا يَحْفَظُ.

Verses and Supplications That Treat Forgetfulness and Assist in Memorization

You should recite the following (verse) ten times:

﴿فَفَهَّمْنَاهَا سُلَيْمَانَ وَكُلًّا آتَيْنَا حُكْمًا وَعِلْمًا وَسَخَّرْنَا مَعَ دَاوُودَ الْجِبَالَ يُسَبِّحْنَ وَالطَّيْرَ وَكُنَّا فَاعِلِينَ﴾

"And We caused Sulaymān to understand it. And to each We gave wisdom and knowledge. And We subjugated with Dāwūd the mountains that glorified (God) and the birds. And We were the doers (of that)."[3]

Afterwards, you should make the following supplication:

يَا حَيُّ يَا قَيُّومُ يَا رَبَّ مُوسَى وَهَارُونَ وَرَبَّ إِبْرَاهِيمَ وَيَا رَبَّ مُحَمَّدٍ صَلَّى اللهُ عَلَيْهِ وَسَلَّمَ وَعَلَيْهِمْ أَجْمَعِينَ ارْزُقْنِي الْفَهْمَ وَارْزُقْنِي الْعِلْمَ وَالْحِكْمَةَ وَالْعَقْلَ بِرَحْمَتِكَ يَا أَرْحَمَ الرَّاحِمِينَ.

"O Living! O Self-Subsistent! O Lord of Mūsā and Hārūn! O Lord of Ibrāhīm! O Lord of Muhammad ﷺ, provide me with understanding and provide me with knowledge, wisdom and intelligence, by Your mercy, O Most Merciful of those who show mercy."

Ibn Masʿūd ؓ related that the Prophet ﷺ said, "If someone fears that he will forget the Qur'an after having memorized it, or knowledge after learning it, he should say (the following):

اللهُمَّ نَوِّرْ بِالْكِتَابِ بَصَرِي وَاشْرَحْ بِهِ صَدْرِي وَاسْتَعْمِلْ بِهِ بَدَنِي وَأَطْلِقْ بِهِ لِسَانِي وَقَوِّ بِهِ جَنَانِي (قَلْبِي) وَاشْرَحْ بِهِ فَهْمِي وَقَوِّ بِهِ عَزْمِي بِحَوْلِكَ وَقُوَّتِكَ فَإِنَّهُ لَا حَوْلَ وَلَا قُوَّةَ إِلَّا بِكَ يَا أَرْحَمَ الرَّاحِمِينَ

3 *al-Anbiyā'*, 79.

آيَاتٌ وَدَعَوَاتٌ تُعَالِجُ النِّسْيَانَ وَتُسَاعِدُ عَلَى الْحِفْظِ

تَقْرَأُ كُلَّ يَوْمٍ عَشْرَ مَرَّاتٍ ﴿فَفَهَّمْنَاهَا سُلَيْمَانَ وَكُلًّا آتَيْنَا حُكْمًا وَعِلْمًا وَسَخَّرْنَا مَعَ دَاوُودَ الْجِبَالَ يُسَبِّحْنَ وَالطَّيْرَ وَكُنَّا فَاعِلِينَ﴾ [الْأَنْبِيَاءُ: ٩٧].

ثُمَّ تَدْعُو: يَا حَيُّ يَا قَيُّومُ يَا رَبَّ مُوسَى وَهَارُونَ وَرَبَّ إِبْرَاهِيمَ، وَيَا رَبَّ مُحَمَّدٍ صَلَّى اللهُ عَلَيْهِ وَسَلَّمَ وَعَلَيْهِمْ أَجْمَعِينَ ارْزُقْنِي الْفَهْمَ وَارْزُقْنِي الْعِلْمَ وَالْحِكْمَةَ وَالْعَقْلَ بِرَحْمَتِكَ يَا أَرْحَمَ الرَّاحِمِينَ.

وَعَنْ ابْنِ مَسْعُودٍ رَضِيَ اللهُ عَنْهُ عَنِ النَّبِيِّ صَلَّى اللهُ عَلَيْهِ وَسَلَّمَ قَالَ: «مَنْ خَشِيَ أَنْ يَنْسَى الْقُرْآنَ بَعْدَ حِفْظِهِ وَالْعِلْمَ بَعْدَ دَرْسِهِ فَلْيَقُلْ: اللَّهُمَّ نَوِّرْ بِالْكِتَابِ بَصَرِي، وَاشْرَحْ بِهِ صَدْرِي، وَاسْتَعْمِلْ بِهِ بَدَنِي، وَأَطْلِقْ بِهِ لِسَانِي، وَقَوِّ بِهِ جَنَانِي (قَلْبِي)، وَاشْرَحْ بِهِ فَهْمِي، وَقَوِّ بِهِ عَزْمِي بِحَوْلِكَ وَقُوَّتِكَ فَإِنَّهُ لَا حَوْلَ وَلَا قُوَّةَ إِلَّا بِكَ يَا أَرْحَمَ الرَّاحِمِينَ».

'O, Allah, illuminate with Your Book my sight, expand through it my breast, employ with it my body, cause it to be pronounced by my tongue, strengthen with it my heart, expand with it my understanding and strengthen with it my resolve, that is, through Your might and power. For indeed there is no might nor power except with You. O Most Merciful of those who show mercy.'"

You should also hold your head after each prayer and recite the following seven times:

﴿سَنُقۡرِئُكَ فَلَا تَنسَىٰٓ﴾

"We shall cause You to recite and you will not forget."[4]

Ibn Sinān related that al-Mughīrah ibn Subayᶜ said, "Whoever recites ten verses from al-Baqarah before sleeping will not forget the Qur'an: four verses from the beginning, Āyah al-Kursī and the two verses that follow it, and three from its end." It was narrated by al-Dārimī.

Recite Fātiḥah al-Kitāb (Sūrah al-Fātiḥah) frequently, for it is the opener of good, felicity, and blessing. For is it not the opening of the Book of Allah and the Speech of Allah? That is why the Messenger of Allah ﷺ said, "The Opening of the Book is a cure for every illness." It was related by al-Dārimī and al-Bayhaqī as a *mursal* narration, on the authority of ᶜAbd al-Malik ibn ᶜUmayr, with a chain whose narrators are all trustworthy.

In addition, another beneficial method for preventing forgetfulness and retaining what one has memorized is repeating this supplication:

اللهُمَّ افْتَحْ عَلَيَّ فُتُوحَ الْعَارِفِينَ بِحِكْمَتِكَ وَانْشُرْ عَلَيَّ رَحْمَتَكَ وَذَكِّرْنِي مَا نَسِيتُ يَا ذَا الْجَلَالِ وَالْإِكْرَامِ

"O Allah, grant me the opening of the gnostics through Your wisdom, spread over me Your mercy, and remind me when I forget, O Owner of majesty and honour."

* * *

4 *al-Aᶜlā*, 6.

وَتُمسِكُ بِيَدِكَ الْيُمْنَى رَأْسَكَ وَتَقْرَأُ عَقِبَ كُلِّ صَلَاةٍ ﴿سَنُقْرِئُكَ فَلَا تَنْسَى﴾ [الْأَعْلَى: ٦] سَبْعَ مَرَّاتٍ.

وَعَنْ ابْنِ سِنَانٍ عَنِ الْمُغِيرَةِ بْنِ سَبِيعٍ قَالَ: مَنْ قَرَأَ عَشْرَ آيَاتٍ مِنَ الْبَقَرَةِ عِنْدَ مَنَامِهِ لَمْ يَنْسَ الْقُرْآنَ: أَرْبَعُ آيَاتٍ مِنْ أَوَّلِهَا، وَآيَةُ الْكُرْسِيِّ وَآيَتَانِ بَعْدَهَا «أَيْ بَعْدَ آيَةِ الْكُرْسِيِّ» وَثَلَاثٌ مِنْ آخِرِهَا «أَيْ مِنْ سُورَةِ الْبَقَرَةِ» أَخْرَجَهُ الدَّارِمِيُّ.

الْإِكْثَارُ مِنْ قِرَاءَةِ فَاتِحَةِ الْكِتَابِ «سُورَةُ الْفَاتِحَةِ» فَهِيَ فَاتِحَةُ الْخَيْرِ وَالسَّعَادَةِ وَالْبَرَكَاتِ، أَلَيْسَتْ هِيَ فَاتِحَةُ كِتَابِ اللهِ وَكَلَامُ اللهِ، وَلِذَا قَالَ رَسُولُ اللهِ صَلَّى اللهُ عَلَيْهِ وَسَلَّمَ: «فَاتِحَةُ الْكِتَابِ شِفَاءٌ مِنْ كُلِّ دَاءٍ» أَخْرَجَهُ الدَّارِمِيُّ وَالْبَيْهَقِيُّ فِي الشُّعَبِ مُرْسَلًا بِسَنَدٍ رِجَالُهُ ثِقَاتٌ عَنْ عَبْدِ الْمَلِكِ بْنِ عُمَيْرٍ.

وَلِعَدَمِ النِّسْيَانِ وَتَثْبِيتِ حِفْظِ الْقُرْآنِ تُكَرِّرُ هَذَا الدُّعَاءَ: اللَّهُمَّ افْتَحْ عَلَيَّ فُتُوحَ الْعَارِفِينَ بِحِكْمَتِكَ، وَانْشُرْ عَلَيَّ رَحْمَتَكَ، وَذَكِّرْنِي مَا نَسِيتُ يَا ذَا الْجَلَالِ وَالْإِكْرَامِ.

* * *

You should also recite this supplication before your lesson:

اللهُمَّ إِنِّي أَسْتَوْدِعُكَ مَا عَلَّمْتَنِيهِ فَارْدُدْهُ إِلَيَّ عِنْدَ حَاجَتِي إِلَيْهِ وَلَا تُنْسِنِيهِ يَا رَبَّ الْعَالَمِينَ، اللهُمَّ أَخْرِجْنَا مِنْ ظُلُمَاتِ الْوَهْمِ وَأَكْرِمْنَا بِنُورِ الْفَهْمِ وَافْتَحْ عَلَيْنَا بِمَعْرِفَةِ الْعِلْمِ وَحَسِّنْ أَخْلَاقَنَا بِالْحِلْمِ وَسَهِّلْ لَنَا أَبْوَابَ فَضْلِكَ وَانْشُرْ عَلَيْنَا مِنْ خَزَائِنِ رَحْمَتِكَ يَا أَرْحَمَ الرَّاحِمِينَ

"O Allah, I entrust to You whatever You teach me, so return it to me at the time that I need it. And do not cause me to forget it, O Lord of all the worlds. O Allah, take us out of the darkness of illusion and honour us with the light of understanding. Open upon us, through gnosis, knowledge. Beautify our conduct with forbearance, and facilitate for us the doors to Your grace. And spread upon us mercy from the treasures of Your mercy, O Most Merciful of those who show mercy." The Qur'an used to be revealed five by five. In other words, five (verses) were revealed in the morning and five in the evening. That is why Imam ʿAlī – may Allah ennoble his countenance – said, "The Qur'an was revealed five by five, all except Sūrah al-Anʿām. Whoever memorizes it five by five will not forget it." It has been said that Sūrah al-Anʿām was revealed entirely in one single episode of revelation. Among that which helps memorization is what many of the pious have recommended, which is the recitation of the following verse when one intends to sleep:

﴿إِنَّ فِي خَلْقِ السَّمَوَاتِ وَالْأَرْضِ وَاخْتِلَافِ اللَّيْلِ وَالنَّهَارِ وَالْفُلْكِ الَّتِي تَجْرِي فِي الْبَحْرِ بِمَا يَنفَعُ النَّاسَ ...﴾

"Indeed, in the creation of the Heavens and the Earth, and the alternation of the night and the day, and in the ship that travels over the sea with that which benefits mankind..."[5] (until the end of the verse).

---

5 *al-Baqarah*, 164.

وَتَقْرَأُ هَذَا الدُّعَاءَ قَبْلَ الدَّرْسِ: «اللَّهُمَّ إِنِّي أَسْتَوْدِعُكَ مَا عَلَّمْتَنِيهِ فَارْدُدْهُ إِلَيَّ عِنْدَ حَاجَتِي إِلَيْهِ، وَلَا تُنْسِنِيهِ يَا رَبَّ الْعَالَمِينَ، اللَّهُمَّ أَخْرِجْنَا مِنْ ظُلُمَاتِ الْوَهْمِ، وَأَكْرِمْنَا بِنُورِ الْفَهْمِ، وَافْتَحْ عَلَيْنَا بِمَعْرِفَةِ الْعِلْمِ وَحَسِّنْ أَخْلَاقَنَا بِالْحِلْمِ، وَسَهِّلْ لَنَا أَبْوَابَ فَضْلِكَ، وَانْشُرْ عَلَيْنَا مِنْ خَزَائِنِ رَحْمَتِكَ يَا أَرْحَمَ الرَّاحِمِينَ».

وَلَا تَنْسَ اسْتِفْتَاحَ الْحِفْظِ بِالصَّلَاةِ عَلَى النَّبِيِّ صَلَّى اللهُ عَلَيْهِ وَسَلَّمَ مَعَ الدُّعَاءِ وَالذِّكْرِ.

كَانَ الْقُرْآنُ يَنْزِلُ خَمْساً خَمْساً «أَيْ خَمْسَ آيَاتٍ بِالْغَدَاةِ وَخَمْساً بِالْعَشِيِّ» وَلِذَا قَالَ الْإِمَامُ عَلِيٌّ كَرَّمَ اللهُ وَجْهَهُ: «أُنْزِلَ الْقُرْآنُ خَمْساً خَمْساً إِلَّا سُورَةَ الْأَنْعَامِ، وَمَنْ حَفِظَ خَمْساً خَمْساً لَمْ يَنْسَهُ». قِيلَ أَنَّ سُورَةَ الْأَنْعَامِ نَزَلَتْ دَفْعَةً وَاحِدَةً.

وَمِمَّا يُعِينُ فِي الْحِفْظِ مَا يُوصِي بِهِ كَثِيرٌ مِنَ الصَّالِحِينَ وَهُوَ: قِرَاءَةُ آيَةِ ﴿إِنَّ فِي خَلْقِ السَّمَوَاتِ وَالْأَرْضِ وَاخْتِلَافِ اللَّيْلِ وَالنَّهَارِ وَالْفُلْكِ الَّتِي تَجْرِي فِي الْبَحْرِ بِمَا يَنفَعُ النَّاسَ ...﴾ إِلَى آخِرِ الْآيَةِ [الْبَقَرَةُ: ١٦٤]، عِنْدَ إِرَادَةِ النَّوْمِ. وَمِمَّا يُسَاعِدُ عَلَى الْحِفْظِ أَنْ يَكُونَ وَقْتُ التَّحْفِيظِ قُبَيْلَ النَّوْمِ لَيْلاً.

And from among the matters which help memorization is knowing that the time one memorizes is just before sleeping at night. However, even more important than all of that is that you must abandon disobedience, both publicly and privately, and both small and great [transgressions]. Imam al-Shāfiʿī complained to his Sheikh Wakīʿ of his weak memory. And he said:

I complained to Wakīʿ of my weak memory,
And he guided me to abandon disobedience,
He informed me that knowledge is a light,
And that the light of Allah is not given to the disobedient.

The Book of Allah is superior to all forms of knowledge and greater than all other lights. As such, you must abandon all acts of disobedience, both small and large. And from the greatest of acts of disobedience is exhibiting jealousy and harbouring malice towards others. From that which assists in reaffirming one's knowledge of the Qur'an and its memorization is to have etiquette with it, to venerate and respect it, and to respect the place in which the Qur'an is recited. Thus, it is an obligation upon you to remain silent during the recitation of the Qur'an, listening, contemplating upon its verses, and pondering over them; you must give the Qur'an its merited veneration when you recite it, memorize it, learn it, and teach it. And it is equally imperative that you have presence of heart and awe when you listen to it or recite it.

Reciting the following prayer upon the Prophet ﷺ frequently is a tried and tested cure for forgetfulness. It consists of the following:

اللهُمَّ صَلِّ وَسَلِّمْ وَبَارِكْ عَلَى سَيِّدِنَا وَمَوْلَانَا مُحَمَّدٍ النُّورِ الْمُذْهِبِ لِلنِّسْيَانِ بِنُورِهِ فِي كُلِّ لَمْحَةٍ وَنَفَسٍ عَدَدَ مَا وَسِعَهُ عِلْمُ اللهِ

"O, Allah, send benedictions, peace, and blessings upon our Leader and Master Muhammad, the light through which every form of forgetfulness is dispelled in every moment and with every breath, as many times as are encompassed by the knowledge of Allah." Another formula that assists towards this same end is to recite and memorize the Qur'an while facing

وَأَهَمُّ مِنْ ذَلِكَ كُلِّهِ: عَلَيْكَ بِتَرْكِ الْمَعَاصِي فِي السِّرِّ وَالْعَلَنِ صَغِيرِهَا وَكَبِيرِهَا، وَقَدْ شَكَى الْإِمَامُ الشَّافِعِيُّ إِلَى شَيْخِهِ وَكِيعٍ سُوءَ حِفْظِهِ فَقَالَ:

شَكَوْتُ إِلَى وَكِيعٍ سُوءَ حِفْظِي فَأَرْشَدَنِي إِلَى تَرْكِ الْمَعَاصِي
وَأَعْلَمَنِي بِأَنَّ الْعِلْمَ نُورٌ وَنُورُ اللهِ لَا يُؤْتَى لِعَاصِي

وَكِتَابُ اللهِ فَوْقَ كُلِّ الْعُلُومِ وَفَوْقَ كُلِّ الْأَنْوَارِ فَعَلَيْكَ بِتَرْكِ الْمَعَاصِي صَغِيرِهَا وَكَبِيرِهَا وَمِنْ أَكْبَرِ الْمَعَاصِي الْحَسَدُ وَالْحِقْدُ عَلَى الْآخَرِينَ. وَمِمَّا يُعِينُ عَلَى ثَبَاتِ الْقُرْآنِ وَحِفْظِهِ التَّأَدُّبُ مَعَ الْقُرْآنِ واحْتِرَامُهُ وَتَعْظِيمُهُ وَتَعْظِيمُ الْمَكَانِ الَّذِي يُقْرَأُ فِيهِ الْقُرْآنُ، فَعَلَيْكَ أَنْ تُنْصِتَ لِلْقُرْآنِ وَتَسْتَمِعَ وَتَتَدَبَّرَ الْآيَاتِ وَتَتَفَكَّرَ فِيهَا، وَأَنْ تُعْطِيَ الْقُرْآنَ اِحْتِرَامَهُ مَعَ قِرَاءَتِكَ لَهُ وَعِنْدَ حِفْظِكَ لَهُ وَعِنْدَ أَخْذِهِ وَعِنْدَ وَضْعِهِ، وَعَلَيْكَ أَيْضاً بِحُضُورِ الْقَلْبِ مَعَ الْخَشْيَةِ عِنْدَ سَمَاعِهِ أَوْ قِرَاءَتِهِ.

الْإِكْثَارُ مِنْ هَذِهِ الصَّلَاةِ عَلَى النَّبِيِّ صَلَّى اللهُ عَلَيْهِ وَسَلَّمَ الْمُجَرَّبَةِ لِلنِّسْيَانِ وَهِيَ «اللَّهُمَّ صَلِّ وَسَلِّمْ وَبَارِكْ عَلَى سَيِّدِنَا وَمَوْلَانَا مُحَمَّدٍ النُّورِ الْمُذْهِبِ لِلنِّسْيَانِ بِنُورِهِ فِي كُلِّ لَمْحَةٍ وَنَفَسٍ عَدَدَ مَا وَسِعَهُ عِلْمُ اللهِ». وَأَيْضاً مِمَّا يُعِينُ عَلَى ذَلِكَ أَنْ تَقْرَأَ وَتَتَحَفَّظَ الْقُرْآنَ وَأَنْتَ مُسْتَقْبِلَ الْقِبْلَةِ، بَلْ فِي جَمِيعِ جَلَسَاتِكَ تُحَاوِلُ أَن تَكُونَ مُسْتَقْبِلَ الْقِبْلَةِ لِأَنَّ اِسْتِقْبَالَ الْقِبْلَةِ مِنْ أَسْبَابِ الْفُتُوحِ. وَمِنْ خَوَاصِّ اِسْمِ اللهِ تَعَالَى «الْمُهَيْمِنُ» مَا ذَكَرَهُ السُّهْرَوَرْدِيُّ أَنَّ مَنْ دَاوَمَ

the Qiblah. Rather, it is imperative that every time you sit, you should attempt to face the Qiblah because maintaining such a posture is one of the means of attaining spiritual openings.

From the special qualities of the special name of Allah ﷻ known as الْمُهَيْمِنُ (The Supreme Protector) is what was highlighted by al-Suhrawardī, namely that whoever recites it consistently will have their memorization strengthened and forgetfulness will depart from him. Likewise, al-Suhrawardī mentioned a similar principle regarding His ﷻ name الْقَيُّومُ (the Self-Subsistent): if a person afflicted with a base intellect recites it 16 times every day in an empty place, Allah will safeguard him from the causes of forgetfulness, and He will strengthen his memory and illuminate his heart. Likewise, when attempting to recall what one has forgot, His ﷻ name الْمُعِيدُ (the One Who returns) is repeated. It proves to be particularly effective when coupled with His ﷻ name الْمُبْدِئُ (the Initiator).

From that which strengthens memory and increases intelligence is the use of the *siwāk* (tooth-stick). Such is the case when one uses it regularly and consistently. From among the mentioned benefits of the *siwāk* is that it increases intelligence and grants eloquence to the tongue. As such, you must use it consistently with a noble intention. One should also avoid overindulging, that is, eating to one's fill. Thus, you must not eat a lot. Rather, you should consume that which satisfies your hunger, since satiety does not help in increasing memory. There is a popular aphorism which states, "*Al-Biṭnah* diminishes intelligence." The term *biṭnah* in this context means satiety. From that which has been effectively tried and tested in producing both understanding and memorization is that you recite al-Fātiḥah 41 times during the pre-dawn hour. Similarly, the recitation of يَا مُبْدِئُ يَا خَالِقُ (O You Who initiates, O You Who creates) 100 times a day is also tried and tested. This was copied from the *ijāzah* and counsel of al-Ḥabīb Sālim ibn ʿAbdullāh al-Shāṭirī (may Allah ﷻ preserve him). From that which is understood from many Sheikhs is that writing on one's hand is from the causes of forgetfulness. As such, you should avoid it. Likewise, we hear from many of them that frequently reading what is written on grave markers brings forth forgetfulness, or that it draws forgetfulness. Furthermore, from that which weakens the memory is engaging in the habit of masturbation. It has many detrimental consequences.

عَلَيْهِ قَوِيَ حِفْظُهُ وَذَهَبَ نِسْيَانُهُ. وَكَذَلِكَ اِسْمُهُ تَعَالَى «الْقَيُّومُ» كَمَا ذَكَرَ السُّهْرَوَرْدِيُّ أَيْضاً: أَنَّهُ إِذَا قَرَأَهُ الْبَلِيدُ فِي كُلِّ يَوْمٍ سِتَّ عَشْرَةَ مَرَّةً فِي مَكَانٍ خَالٍ فَإِنَّ اللهَ يُؤَمِّنُهُ مِنْ عَوَارِضِ النِّسْيَانِ وَيُقَوِّي حِفْظَهُ وَيُنَوِّرُ قَلْبَهُ. وَكَذَلِكَ اِسْمُهُ تَعَالَى «الْمُعِيدُ» يُكَرِّرُ مِرَاراً لِتِذْكَارِ الْمَحْفُوظِ إِذَا نُسِيَ لَاسِيَّمَا إِذَا أُضِيفَ إِلَيْهِ اِسْمُهُ تَعَالَى «الْمُبْدِئُ». وَمِمَّا يُقَوِّي الْحَافِظَةَ وَيُقَوِّي الْفِطْنَةَ: السِّوَاكُ.. وَيَكُونُ ذَلِكَ مَعَ الْمُوَاظَبَةِ وَالْاِسْتِمْرَارِ عَلَيْهِ، فَقَدْ عُدَّ مِنْ فَوَائِدِ السِّوَاكِ: أَنَّهُ يُقَوِّي الْفِطْنَةَ وَيُطْلِقُ اللِّسَانَ ... فَعَلَيْكَ بِهِ مَعَ الْمُوَاظَبَةِ وَحُسْنِ النِّيَّةِ. وَعَدَمُ الْإِفْرَاطِ فِي الْأَكْلِ «الشِّبَعُ» فَعَلَيْكَ أَنْ لَا تَأْكُلَ كَثِيراً وَإِنَّمَا تَأْكُلُ الَّذِي يَسُدُّ جُوعَكَ لِأَنَّ الشِّبَعَ لَا يُسَاعِدُ عَلَى تَقْوِيَةِ الْحَافِظَةِ.. وَهُنَاكَ مَقَالَةٌ تَقُولُ: الْبِطْنَةُ تُذْهِبُ الْفِطْنَةَ. الْبِطْنَةُ أَيِ الشِّبَعُ. وَمِمَّا جُرِّبَ لِحُصُولِ الْفَهْمِ وَالْحِفْظِ أَنْ يَقْرَأَ الْفَاتِحَةَ يَوْمِياً وَقْتَ السَّحَرِ (١٤) مَرَّةً وَكَذَلِكَ يَقْرَأُ «يَا مُبْدِئُ يَا خَالِقُ» يَوْمِيّاً مِائَةَ مَرَّةٍ «مَنْقُولَةٌ مِنْ إِجَازَةِ وَوَصِيَّةِ الْحَبِيبِ: سَالِمُ بْنُ عَبْدِ اللهِ الشَّاطِرِيُّ حَفِظَهُ اللهُ تَعَالَى». وَمِمَّا نَسْمَعُ مِنْ كَثِيرٍ مِنَ الشُّيُوخِ أَنَّ الْكِتَابَةَ عَلَى الْيَدِ مِنْ أَسْبَابِ النِّسْيَانِ فَابْتَعِدْ عَنْهَا. كَذَلِكَ نَسْمَعُ مِنْهُمْ أَنَّ إِكْثَارَ قِرَاءَةِ الْكِتَابَةِ الَّتِي عَلَى شَوَاهِدِ الْقُبُورِ تَزِيدُ فِي النِّسْيَانِ أَوْ أَنَّهَا تَجْلِبُ النِّسْيَانَ. وَمِمَّا يُضْعِفُ الذَّاكِرَةَ «مُمَارَسَةُ الْعَادَةِ السِّرِّيَّةِ» وَلَهَا أَضْرَارٌ كَثِيرَةٌ.

The Prayer for Memorization of the Qur'an and Its Supplication

Ibn ʿAbbās رضي الله عنهما said, "While we were in the presence of the Messenger of Allah ﷺ, ʿAlī رضي الله عنه came and said, 'May my father and mother be ransomed for you, O Messenger of Allah, this Qur'an escapes from my heart. And I do not find myself capable [of keeping] it.' The Messenger of Allah ﷺ responded, 'O Abū al-Ḥasan, should I not teach you some words by which Allah will benefit you, and by which He will also benefit those to whom you teach them?' He replied, 'Yes, O Messenger of Allah!' He said, 'On the eve of Friday, if you are able to stand in the last third of the night then do so, for that is the witnessed hour, and supplication in it is answered. Indeed, my brother Yaʿqūb said to his sons: "I shall seek forgiveness for you from my Lord."[6] He was making reference to the eve of Friday. However, if you are unable, then stand in the middle of that night. If you are unable to do that, then stand at its beginning. And pray four *rakʿahs*. In the first *rakʿah*, recite Sūrah al-Fātiḥah and Sūrah Yā Sīn, in the second *rakʿah*, recite Sūrah al-Fātiḥah and Sūrah Ḥā' Mīm al-Dukhān, in the third *rakʿah*, recite Sūrah al-Fātiḥah and Sūrah Alif-Lām-Mīm al-Sajdah, and in the fourth *rakʿah* recite Sūrah al-Fātiḥah and Sūrah al-Mulk. After you have completed that prayer, you should praise Allah and extol Him in an excellent manner. Then, you should send prayers upon me and upon all the Prophets in an excellent manner. Afterwards, you should seek forgiveness for the male and female believers and for your brethren who have preceded you in faith. After that, you should say:

اللهُمَّ ارْحَمْنِي بِتَرْكِ الْمَعَاصِي أَبَداً مَا أَبْقَيْتَنِي وَارْحَمْنِي أَنْ أَتَكَلَّفَ مَا لَا يَعْنِينِي وَارْزُقْنِي حُسْنَ النَّظَرِ فِيمَا يُرْضِيكَ عَنِّي. اللهُمَّ بَدِيعَ السَّمَوَاتِ وَالْأَرْضِ يَا ذَا الْجَلَالِ وَالْإِكْرَامِ وَالْعِزَّةِ الَّتِي لَا تُرَامُ أَسْأَلُكَ يَا اللهُ يَا رَحْمَنُ بِجَلَالِكَ وَنُورِ

---

6 *Yūsuf*, 98.

صَلاَةُ حِفْظِ الْقُرآنِ وَدُعَاؤُهَا

عَنْ ابْنِ عَبَّاسٍ رَضِيَ اللهُ عَنْهُمَا قَالَ: «بَيْنَمَا نَحْنُ عِنْدَ رَسُولِ اللهِ صَلَّى اللهُ عَلَيْهِ وَسَلَّمَ إِذْ جَاءَهُ عَلِيٌّ رَضِيَ اللهُ عَنْهُ فَقَالَ: بِأَبِي أَنْتَ وَأُمِّي يَا رَسُولَ اللهِ .. تَفَلَّتَ هَذَا الْقُرآنُ مِنْ صَدْرِي فَمَا أَجِدُنِي أَقْدِرُ عَلَيْهِ فَقَالَ رَسُولُ اللهِ صَلَّى اللهُ عَلَيْهِ وَسَلَّمَ يَا أَبَا الْحَسَنِ أَفَلاَ أُعَلِّمُكَ كَلِمَاتٍ يَنْفَعُكَ اللهُ بِهِنَّ، وَيَنْفَعُ بِهِنَّ مَنْ عَلَّمْتَهُ، وَيُثَبِّتُ مَا تَعَلَّمْتَ فِي صَدْرِكَ؟ قَالَ: أَجَلْ يَا رَسُولَ اللهِ فَعَلِّمْنِي، قَالَ: إِذَا كَانَ لَيلَةَ الْجُمُعَةِ فَإِنْ اسْتَطَعْتَ أَنْ تَقُومَ فِي ثُلُثِ اللَّيْلِ الْآخِرِ فَإِنَّهَا سَاعَةٌ مَشْهُودَةٌ وَالدُّعَاءُ فِيهَا مُسْتَجَابٌ، وَقَدْ قَالَ أَخِي يَعْقُوبُ لِبَنِيهِ ﴿سَوْفَ أَسْتَغْفِرُ لَكُمْ رَبِّي﴾ يَقُولُ حَتَّى تَأْتِي لَيْلَةُ الْجُمُعَةِ، فَإِنْ لَمْ تَسْتَطِعْ فَقُمْ فِي وَسَطِهَا فَإِنْ لَمْ تَسْتَطِعْ فَقُمْ فِي أَوَّلِهَا، فَصَلِّ أَرْبَعَ رَكَعَاتٍ تَقْرَأُ فِي الرَّكْعَةِ الْأُولَى بِفَاتِحَةِ الْكِتَابِ وَسُورَةِ يس، وَالرَّكْعَةِ الثَّانِيَّةِ: بِفَاتِحَةِ الْكِتَابِ وَحم - الدُّخَانِ - وَفِي الرَّكْعَةِ الثَّالِثَةِ: بِفَاتِحَةِ الْكِتَابِ وَالَمَ تَنْزِيلُ - السَّجْدَةِ - وَفِي الرَّكْعَةِ الرَّابِعَةِ: بِفَاتِحَةِ الْكِتَابِ وَتَبَارَكَ الْمُلْكِ - فَإِذَا فَرَغْتَ مِنَ التَّشَهُّدِ فَاحْمَدِ اللهَ وَأَحْسِنِ الثَّنَاءَ عَلَى اللهِ وَصَلِّ عَلَيَّ وَأَحْسِنْ وَعَلَى سَائِرِ النَّبِيِّينَ وَاسْتَغْفِرْ لِلْمُؤْمِنِينَ وَالْمُؤْمِنَاتِ وَلِإِخْوَانِكَ الَّذِينَ سَبَقُوكَ بِالْإِيمَانِ. **ثُمَّ قُلْ فِي آخِرِ ذَلِكَ:** اللَّهُمَّ ارْحَمْنِي بِتَرْكِ الْمَعَاصِي أَبَداً مَا أَبْقَيْتَنِي وَارْحَمْنِي أَنْ أَتَكَلَّفَ مَا لَا يَعْنِينِي وَارْزُقْنِي حُسْنَ النَّظَرِ فِيمَا يُرْضِيكَ عَنِّي. اللَّهُمَّ بَدِيعَ السَّمَوَاتِ وَالْأَرْضِ يَا ذَا الْجَلَالِ وَالْإِكْرَامِ وَالْعِزَّةِ الَّتِي لَا تُرَامُ أَسْأَلُكَ يَا اللهُ يَا رَحْمَنُ بِجَلَالِكَ وَنُورِ وَجْهِكَ أَنْ تُنَوِّرَ بِكِتَابِكَ بَصَرِي، وَأَنْ تُطْلِقَ بِهِ لِسَانِي، وَأَنْ تَفَرِّجَ بِهِ عَنْ

وَجْهِكَ أَنْ تُنَوِّرَ بِكِتَابِكَ بَصَرِي وَأَنْ تُطْلِقَ بِهِ لِسَانِي وَأَنْ تَفَرَّجَ بِهِ عَنْ قَلْبِي وَأَنْ تَشْرَحَ بِهِ صَدْرِي وَأَنْ تُعْمِلَ بِهِ بَدَنِي لِأَنَّهُ لَا يُعِينُنِي عَلَى الْحَقِّ غَيْرُكَ وَلَا يُؤْتِينِيهِ إِلَّا أَنْتَ وَلَا حَوْلَ وَلَا قُوَّةَ إِلَّا بِاللهِ الْعَلِيِّ الْعَظِيمِ

O, Allah, bless me with the everlasting abandonment of disobedience as long as You keep me alive. Bless me with leaving that which does not concern me. Bless me with an excellent vision of that which will make You satisfied with me. O Allah, O Originator of the Heavens and the Earth, O Owner of majesty and honour, and never-ending might! I ask you, O Allah, O Most Merciful, through Your majesty and the light of Your countenance, to illuminate with Your Book my sight, to cause my tongue to pronounce it, to grant relief through my heart, to expand with it my breast, and to cause my body to put it in practice, because none can help me in the truth except You. Nor can I attain it except through You. There is no might nor power except in Allah, the Exalted, the Great.

O Abū al-Ḥasan, do that for three, five, or seven Fridays. You will be granted your request with the permission of Allah. By the One Who has sent me with the truth, it will never fail any believer.'"

قَلْبِي، وَأَنْ تَشْرَحَ بِهِ صَدْرِي، وَأَنْ تُعْمِلَ بِهِ بَدَنِي لِأَنَّهُ لَا يُعِينُنِي عَلَى الْحَقِّ غَيْرُكَ وَلَا يُؤْتِينِيهِ إِلَّا أَنْتَ وَلَا حَوْلَ وَلَا قُوَّةَ إِلَّا بِاللهِ الْعَلِيِّ الْعَظِيمِ «يَا أَبَا الْحَسَنِ فَافْعَلْ ذَلِكَ ثَلَاثَ جُمَعٍ أَوْ خَمْساً أَوْ سَبْعاً تُجَابُ بِإِذْنِ اللهِ، وَالَّذِي بَعَثَنِي بِالْحَقِّ مَا أَخْطَأَ مُؤْمِناً قَطُّ».

A Supplication for Memorizing the Qur'an

O, Allah, I ask you, O Allah, by the truth of the secret which You deposited in the heart of Your Prophet Muhammad ﷺ, and by the spirit of Your secret which is found in the spirits of Your saints, and by the wondrous manifestations of Your gentle mercy and decrees, and Your subtle workmanship in Your creations, and by the astounding, fantastic wisdom in all Your works, that You make my form elevated and adorned, and ready to receive the insightful conceptualizations that correspond to the unique forms. And make me a bearer of the secret of the Qur'an, O Granter of requests, and allow me to be attributed with the secret of the Criterion. And make me eloquent in speech. Beautify my inner being with the light of Oneness. And confer upon me the lights of Your manifestations. O Allah, none can prevent what You have given, and none can give what you have withheld. O Most Forgiving, I ask You, by Your beginning-less might and by Your eternal power, that You grant me the coolness of Your pardon on the Day of Gathering, and the sweetness of Your forgiveness on the Day of revealing of worry, sorrows and happiness. O, Allah, make me firm in faith through the unveiling of Your light. Indeed, You are Allah, the Light, Curer of hearts, O Most Forgiving. I ask You, O Allah, by the subtleties of Your hidden, gentle mercy, and Your all-encompassing generosity, that You make my soul busy with all kinds of worship, my spirit filled with the secrets of gnosis, and my heart attributed with the realities and beauty of Your names of attributes. My Lord, make my feet firm in Your obedience until I never slip upon the Path, O Most Merciful of those who show mercy. Illuminate my heart with Your gnosis, and busy me with the recitation of Your Qur'an. Grant me insight just as You granted insight to Your Saints, until I attain the service of the Poles and the Saints. For in their service does the perfection, elevation, and beauty lie. O Allah, I beseech You for a secret from Your secret, a command from Your commands, and a light from Your lights. Grant me and cause me to attain Your satisfaction and their satisfaction, through Your satisfaction, O Most Merciful of those who show mercy. May Allah bless our Master Muhammad, his family, and Companions and grant them peace.

دُعَاءٌ لِحِفْظِ الْقُرْآنِ

اللَّهُمَّ إِنِّي أَسْأَلُكَ يَا اللهُ بِحَقِّ سِرِّكَ الْمَوْدُوعِ فِي قَلْبِ نَبِيِّكَ مُحَمَّدٍ صَلَّى اللهُ عَلَيْهِ وَسَلَّمَ وَبِرُوحِ سِرِّكَ الْمَوْجُودِ فِي رُوحِ أَوْلِيَائِكَ وَبَدَائِعِ لُطْفِكَ فِي مَقْدُورَاتِكَ وَدَقَائِقِ إِتْقَانِكَ فِي مُخْتَرَعَاتِكَ وَبِعَجَائِبِ غَرَائِبِ حِكْمَتِكَ فِي مَصْنُوعَاتِكَ أَنْ تَجْعَلَ صُورَتِي مَنْسُوبَةً وَمُتَخَلِّيَةً، مُسْتَعِدَّةً لِاكْتِسَابِ الصُّوَرِ الْعِلْمِيَّةِ الْمُطَابِقَةِ لِلصُّوَرِ الْوَحْدَانِيَّةِ، وَاجْعَلْنِي حَامِلاً سِرَّ الْقُرْآنِ يَا مُجِيبُ، مَوْصُوفًا بِأَوْصَافِ سِرِّ الْفُرْقَانِ، وَاخْتَرِعْنِي بِانْطِلَاقِ اللِّسَانِ، وَزَيِّنْ بَاطِنِي بِنُورِ التَّوْحِيدِ وَاخْلَعْ عَلَيَّ أَنْوَارَ تَجَلِّيَاتِكَ. اللَّهُمَّ لَا مَانِعَ لِمَا أَعْطَيْتَ وَلَا مُعْطِيَ لِمَا مَنَعْتَ، يَا غَفَّارُ أَسْأَلُكَ بِقُدْرَتِكَ الْقَدِيمَةِ وَبِقُوَّتِكَ الْقَوِيمَةِ أَنْ تَرْزُقَنِي بَرْدَ عَفْوِكَ يَوْمَ الْمَحْشَرِ وَحَلَاوَةَ مَغْفِرَتِكَ يَوْمَ ظُهُورِ الْهَمِّ وَالْحُزْنِ وَالسُّرُورِ. اللَّهُمَّ ثَبِّتْنِي عَلَى الْإِيمَانِ لِانْكِشَافِ نُورِكَ إِنَّكَ أَنْتَ اللهُ النُّورُ شَافِي الصُّدُورِ يَا غَفَّارُ أَسْأَلُكَ يَا اللهُ بِدَقَائِقِ لُطْفِكَ الْخَفِيِّ وَإِحْسَانِكَ الْوَفِيِّ أَنْ تَجْعَلَ نَفْسِي بِأَنْوَاعِ الْعِبَادَةِ مَعْمُورَةً وَرُوحِي بِأَسْرَارِ الْمَعَارِفِ مَنْشُورَةً وَقَلْبِي بِحَقَائِقِ رَوَائِقِ أَسْمَاءِ صِفَاتِكَ مَوْصُوفاً، إِلَهِي ثَبِّتْ قَدَمِي عَلَى طَاعَتِكَ حَتَّى لَا أَزِلَّ عَلَى الصِّرَاطِ يَا أَرْحَمَ الرَّاحِمِينَ، وَنَوِّرْ قَلْبِي بِمَعْرِفَتِكَ، وَاشْغَلْنِي بِتِلَاوَةِ الْقُرْآنِ، وَبَصِّرْنِي كَمَا بَصَّرْتَ أَوْلِيَاءَكَ حَتَّى أَنَالَ خِدْمَةَ الْأَقْطَابِ وَالْأَوْلِيَاءِ فَفِي خِدْمَتِهِمْ دَرْجُ الْكَمَالِ وَالرِّفْعَةِ وَالْجَمَالِ، اللَّهُمَّ إِنِّي أَسْأَلُكَ سِرّاً مِنْ سِرِّكَ وَأَمْراً مِنْ أَمْرِكَ وَنُوراً مِنْ نُورِكَ، وَنَوِّلْنِي وَأَوْصِلْنِي لِرِضَاكَ وَرِضَاهُمْ بِرِضَاكَ يَا أَرْحَمَ الرَّاحِمِينَ وَصَلَّى اللهُ عَلَى سَيِّدِنَا مُحَمَّدٍ وَعَلَى آلِهِ وَصَحْبِهِ وَسَلَّمَ.

Various Beneficial Formulas

A beneficial formula for openings: Al-Ghazālī ﵀ said, "Among the means of swift memorization is maintaining consistency in acts of obedience, leaving disobedience, using the *siwāk*, abandoning sleep, praying at night, reciting the Qur'an while looking at the physical page directly, drinking honey, eating sweetened ginger, and eating 21 grapes on an empty stomach."

For strengthening memorization: One should recite these two verses:

﴿وَلَوْ أَنَّمَا فِي الْأَرْضِ مِن شَجَرَةٍ أَقْلَامٌ وَالْبَحْرُ يَمُدُّهُ مِن بَعْدِهِ سَبْعَةُ أَبْحُرٍ مَّا نَفِدَتْ كَلِمَاتُ اللَّهِ إِنَّ اللَّهَ عَزِيزٌ حَكِيمٌ ﴿٢٧﴾ مَّا خَلْقُكُمْ وَلَا بَعْثُكُمْ إِلَّا كَنَفْسٍ وَاحِدَةٍ إِنَّ اللَّهَ سَمِيعٌ بَصِيرٌ﴾

"And if all the trees on Earth were pens, and the sea were their ink, along with seven other seas, the words of Allah would never be exhausted. Indeed, Allah is Almighty, All-Wise. Your creation and your being brought back are but like a single soul. Indeed, Allah is All-Hearing, All-Seeing."[7]

A beneficial formula for the one who has a slow mind: You should recite the *basmalāh* for him 786 times and then blow it into water. Then you should give it to him to drink for seven days on an empty stomach. Alternatively, you may write Sūrah Yā Sīn with musk and saffron, followed by dissolving it in rose water and giving it to him to drink over seven consecutive days. He will remember whatever he hears with the permission of Allah. Additionally, if the name of Allah الوَهَّابُ (the Giver) is written and dissolved and then given to drink to a person who has a sluggish mind, Allah will facilitate for him understanding and memorization, and He will open for Him the riches of hidden bestowal.

A beneficial formula for forgetfulness: If someone studies and forgets, he should recite every day the following two verses 100 times apiece:

---

7 *Luqmān*, 27-28.

فَوَائِدُ

فَائِدَةٌ لِلْفُتُوحِ: قَالَ الْغَزَالِيُّ رَحِمَهُ اللّٰهُ: مِنْ أَسْبَابِ سُرْعَةِ الْحِفْظِ: الْمُوَاظَبَةُ عَلَى الطَّاعَةِ، وَتَرْكُ الْمَعَاصِي، وَاسْتِعْمَالُ السِّوَاكِ، وَتَرْكُ النَّوْمِ، وَصَلَاةُ اللَّيْلِ، وَقِرَاءَةُ الْقُرْآنِ نَظَراً، وَشُرْبُ الْعَسَلِ، وَأَكْلُ الْكَنْدَرِ مَعَ السُّكَّرِ، وَأَكْلُ إِحْدَى وَعِشْرِينَ زَبِيبَةً حَمْرَاءَ عَلَى الرِّيقِ.

لِتَقْوِيَةِ الذَّاكِرَةِ: يَقْرَأُ هَاتَانِ الْآيَتَانِ: ﴿وَلَوْ أَنَّمَا فِي الْأَرْضِ مِن شَجَرَةٍ أَقْلَامٌ وَالْبَحْرُ يَمُدُّهُ مِن بَعْدِهِ سَبْعَةُ أَبْحُرٍ مَّا نَفِدَتْ كَلِمَاتُ اللَّهِ إِنَّ اللَّهَ عَزِيزٌ حَكِيمٌ * مَّا خَلْقُكُمْ وَلَا بَعْثُكُمْ إِلَّا كَنَفْسٍ وَاحِدَةٍ إِنَّ اللَّهَ سَمِيعٌ بَصِيرٌ﴾. [سُورَةُ لُقْمَانَ: ٧٢/٨٢]

فَائِدَةٌ لِبَلِيدِ الذِّهْنِ: يَقْرَأُ لَهُ الْبَسْمَلَةَ (٦٨٧) مَرَّةً عَلَى قَدَحِ مَاءٍ وَيَسْقِيهِ عَلَى الرِّيقِ عَلَى سَبْعَةِ أَيَّامٍ. أَوْ يَكْتُبُ لَهُ سُورَةَ يٰسٓ بِمِسْكٍ وَزَعْفَرَانٍ وَيَمْحُوهَا بِمَاءِ الْوَرْدِ وَيَسْقِيهِ إِيَّاهَا سَبْعَةَ أَيَّامٍ مُتَوَالِيَةٍ فَإِنَّهُ يَحْفَظُ كُلَّ مَا يَسْمَعُهُ بِإِذْنِ اللّٰهِ. وَإِسْمُ اللّٰهِ الْوَهَّابُ إِذَا كُتِبَ وَمُحِيَ بِالْمَاءِ وَشَرِبَهُ بَلِيدُ الذِّهْنِ سَهَّلَ اللّٰهُ لَهُ الْفَهْمَ وَالْحِفْظَ وَيَفْتَحُ لَهُ مِنْ خَزَائِنِ الْغَيْبِ الْوَهْبِيَّةِ.

فَائِدَةٌ لِلنِّسْيَانِ: مَنْ كَانَ يَتَعَلَّمُ وَيَنْسَى فَلْيَقْرَأْ كُلَّ يَوْمٍ مِائَةَ مَرَّةٍ هَاتَيْنِ الْآيَتَيْنِ

﴿وَتَعِيَهَا أُذُنٌ وَاعِيَةٌ﴾ ﴿سَنُقْرِئُكَ فَلَا تَنسَىٰ﴾

"The attentive ear will memorize it."[8] And: "We will cause you to recite it and you will not forget."[9] Jābir ﷺ said, "When His ﷻ words 'Attentive ears will memorize it' were revealed, he ﷺ said to ʿAlī ﷺ, 'I asked my Lord to make it your ear, O ʿAlī.'" Makḥūl ﷺ said, "ʿAlī used to say, 'I never heard anything from the Messenger of Allah and then forgot it. And I would never forget it.'"

Al-Shādhilī ﷺ said, "Whoever writes these names and then drinks them on an empty stomach will not forget. Whoever recites them over water and washes his face with them, he will never go blind. And whoever writes them and drinks them will not be impotent. They are ʿUthmān ibn ʿAffān, Muʿādh ibn Jabal, ʿAbd al-Raḥmān ibn ʿAwf, Zayd ibn Thābit, Ubayy ibn Kaʿb, Ṭalḥah ibn ʿUbaydullāh and Tamīm al-Dārı ﷺ."

Sheikh ʿAbd al-Salām al-Marrākashī ﷺ said, "Whoever writes the following couplets on a piece of paper and then dissolves it in water and drinks it on an empty stomach for five days, then he will never hear anything after that except that he will memorize it. And he will never forget it through the aid of Allah and His facilitation. They are the following:

لَا تُنْكِرِ الْوَحْيَ مِنْ رُؤْيَاهُ إِنَّ لَهُ * قلباً إذا نَامَتِ العَيْنَانِ لَمْ يَنَمِ

Do not deny the revelation in his dreams, for he,
Has a heart that – when eyes sleep – does not sleep,

وَذَاكَ حِينَ بُلُوغٍ مِنْ نُبُوَّتِهِ * فَلَيْسَ يُنْكِرُ فِيهِ حَالُ مُحْتَلِمٍ

That happened from when he attained maturity, from his Prophecy,
Thus, it is not denied for him during his dream states."

---

8 *al-Ḥāqqah*, 12.

9 *al-Aʿlā*, 6.

وَهُمَا: ﴿وَتَعِيَهَا أُذُنٌ وَاعِيَةٌ﴾ [سُورَةُ الْحَاقَّةِ: ٢١]، ﴿سَنُقْرِئُكَ فَلَا تَنسَىٰ﴾ [سُورَةُ الْأَعْلَى: ٦]. عَنْ جَابِرٍ رَضِيَ اللهُ عَنْهُ قَالَ: لَمَّا نَزَلَ قَوْلُهُ تَعَالَى: ﴿وَتَعِيَهَا أُذُنٌ وَاعِيَةٌ﴾ قَالَ صَلَّى اللهُ عَلَيْهِ وَسَلَّمَ لِعَلِيٍّ: «سَأَلْتُ رَبِّي أَنْ يَجْعَلَهَا أُذُنَكَ يَا عَلِيُّ. قَالَ مَكْحُولٌ رَضِيَ اللهُ عَنْهُ: فَكَانَ عَلِيٌّ يَقُولُ: مَا سَمِعْتُ مِنْ رَسُولِ اللهِ شَيْئاً فَنَسِيتُهُ وَمَا كَانَ لِي أَنْ أَنْسَى». أَخْرَجَهُ ابْنُ جُرَيْجٍ عَنْ عَلِيٍّ.

قَالَ الشَّاذِلِيُّ رَحِمَهُ اللهُ: مَنْ كَتَبَ هَذِهِ الْأَسْمَاءَ وَشَرِبَهَا عَلَى الرِّيقِ لَا يَنْسَى، وَمَنْ قَرَأَهَا عَلَى مَاءٍ وَغَسَلَ بِهَا وَجْهَهُ فَإِنَّهُ لَا يَعْمَى، وَمَنْ كَتَبَهَا وَشَرِبَهَا لَا يَعْجِزُ عَنِ النِّسَاءِ وَهُمْ: عُثْمَانُ بْنُ عَفَّانٍ، مُعَاذُ بْنُ جَبَلٍ، عَبْدُ الرَّحْمَنِ بْنُ عَوْفٍ، زَيْدُ بْنُ ثَابِتٍ، أُبَيُّ بْنُ كَعْبٍ، طَلْحَةُ بْنُ عَبْدِ اللهِ، تَمِيمٌ الدَّارِيُّ رَضِيَ اللهُ عَنْهُمْ.

وَقَالَ الشَّيْخُ عَبْدُ السَّلَامِ الْمُرَّاكُشِيُّ رَحِمَهُ اللهُ: إِنَّ مَنْ كَتَبَ هَذَيْنِ الْبَيْتَيْنِ فِي وَرَقَةٍ وَمَحَاهَا بِالْمَاءِ وَشَرِبَهَا عَلَى الرِّيقِ خَمْسَةَ أَيَّامٍ فَإِنَّهُ لَا يَسْمَعُ بَعْدَ ذَلِكَ شَيْئاً إِلَّا حَفِظَهُ وَلَمْ يَنْسَهُ أَبَداً بِعَوْنِ اللهِ وَقُوَّتِهِ وَهُمَا:

لَا تُنْكِرُ الْوَحْيَ مِنْ رُؤْيَاهُ إِنَّ لَهُ

قلباً إذا نَامَتِ العَيْنَانِ لَمْ يَنَمِ

وَذَاكَ حِينَ بُلُوغٍ مِنْ نُبُوَّتِهِ

فَلَيْسَ يُنْكِرُ فِيهِ حَالُ مُحْتَلِمِ

Al-Nawawī ﷺ said, "If someone frequently forgets what he learns, then let him recite frequently: يَا مُبْدِئُ يَا مُعِيدُ (O, Initiator, O You Who returns). And whoever intends to begin studying the sciences, or any other matter, let him recite يَا مُبْدِئُ156 times. He will be blessed in whatever endeavour he initiates."

A **beneficial formula for memorizing the Qur'an**: al-Shādhilī ﷺ said, "Reciting these stanzas before beginning one's memorization of the Qur'an constitutes a means for facilitating its memorization and solidifying it in one's mind with the permission of Allah. They are:

كَلَامٌ قَدِيمٌ لَا يُمَلُّ سَمَاعُهُ * تَنَزَّهَ عَنْ قَوْلٍ وَفِعْلٍ وَنِيَّةٍ

Beginning less Speech whose hearer is never wearied,
It is transcendent beyond any word, act, or intention,

بِهِ اَشْتَفِي مِنْ كُلِّ دَاءٍ وَنُورُهُ * دَلِيلٌ لِعَقْلِي عِنْدَ جَهْلِي وَحَيْرَتِي

Through it, I seek the cure for every illness and its light,
Is a proof of my intellect, in my ignorance and bewilderment,

فَيَا رَبِّ مَتِّعْنِي بِسِرِّ حُرُوفِهِ * وَنَوِّرْ بِهِ عَقْلِي وَسَمْعِي وَمُقْلَتِي

Thus, my Lord, delight me with the secret of its letters,
And illuminate with it my intellect, my hearing and my eye."

Sheikh ʿAbd al-Salām ﷺ said, "Whoever recites the Qur'an yet is old and finds that it escapes him, then he should write the following couplets on paper with saffron. Then, he should hang it from his neck with a thread, ensuring that the amulet reaches the edge of his chest and is at the end of the thread. Whoever does that will be able to memorize the Qur'an in less than a year through Allah's facilitation. The couplets are as follows:

آيَاتُ حَقٍّ مِنَ الرَّحْمَنِ مُحْدَثَةٌ * قَدِيمَةٌ صِفَةُ الْمَوْصُوفِ بِالْقِدَمِ

Verses of Truth that emerged from the Most Merciful,
Being beginning-less, ascribed with a perpetual eternity,

قَالَ النَّوَوِيُّ رَحِمَهُ اللهُ: مَنْ كَانَ يَنْسَى مَا يَتَعَلَّمُهُ فَلْيُكْثِرْ مِنْ قَوْلِهِ: يَا مُبْدِئُ يَا مُعِيدُ. وَمَنْ أَرَادَ الْاِبْتِدَاءَ بِتَأْلِيفِ الْعُلُومِ أَوْ اِبْتِدَاءً بِأَمْرٍ فَلْيَقُلْ يَا مُبْدِئُ (٦٥) مَرَّةً فَإِنَّهُ يَكُونُ مُبَارَكاً بِكُلِّ مَا ابْتَدَأَ بِهِ.

فَائِدَةٌ لِحِفْظِ الْقُرْآنِ: قَالَ الشَّاذِلِيُّ رَضِيَ اللهُ عَنْهُ: إِنَّ قِرَاءَةَ هَذِهِ الْأَبْيَاتِ قَبْلَ الْبَدْءِ بِحِفْظِ الْقُرْآنِ سَبَبٌ لِتَيْسِيرِ الْحِفْظِ وَثَبَاتِهِ فِي الذِّهْنِ بِإِذْنِ اللهِ وَهِيَ:

كَلَامٌ قَدِيمٌ لَا يُمَلُّ سَمَاعُهُ

تَنَزَّهَ عَنْ قَوْلٍ وَفِعْلٍ وَنِيَّةٍ

بِهِ اَشْتَفِي مِنْ كُلِّ دَاءٍ وَنُورُهُ

دَلِيلٌ لِعَقْلِي عِنْدَ جَهْلِي وَحَيْرَتِي

فَيَا رَبِّ مَتِّعْنِي بِسِرِّ حُرُوفِهِ

وَنَوِّرْ بِهِ عَقْلِي وَسَمْعِي وَمُقْلَتِي

وَقَالَ الشَّيْخُ عَبْدُ السَّلَامِ رَحِمَهُ اللهُ: مَنْ كَانَ يَقْرَأُ الْقُرْآنَ وَهُوَ كَبِيرٌ يَتَفَلَّتُ مِنْهُ فَلْيَكْتُبْ هَذِهِ الْأَبْيَاتَ فِي وَرَقَةٍ بِزَعْفَرَانٍ وَيُعَلِّقُهُ فِي عُنُقِهِ بِخَيْطٍ وَيَكُونُ الْحِرْزُ يَصِلُ إِلَى طَرَفِ صَدْرِهِ فِي طَرَفِ الْخَيْطِ فَإِنَّ الْفَاعِلَ لِذَلِكَ يَحْفَظُ كِتَابَ اللهِ فِي أَقَلَّ مِنْ عَامٍ وَبِاللهِ التَّوْفِيقُ، وَالْأَبْيَاتُ هِيَ:

آيَاتُ حَقٍّ مِنَ الرَّحْمَنِ مُحْدَثَةٌ

قَدِيمَةٌ صِفَةُ الْمَوْصُوفِ بِالْقِدَمِ

لَمْ تَقْتَرِنْ بِزَمَانٍ وَهْيَ تُخْبِرُنَا * عَنِ الْمَعَادِ وَعَنْ عَادٍ وَعَنْ إِرَمِ

They are not restricted to any time. They inform us,
About the final return, of ʿĀd and of Iram,

دَامَتْ لَدَيْنَا فَفَاقَتْ كُلَّ مُعْجِزَةٍ * مِنَ النَّبِيِّينَ إِذْ جَاءَتْ وَلَمْ تَدُمِ

They stayed among us, so they surpassed every miracle,
Of the Prophets which came and did not endure,

مُحَكَّمَاتٌ فَمَا تُبْقِينَ مِنْ شُبَهٍ * لِذِي شِقَاقٍ وَمَا تَبْغِينَ مِنْ حَكَمِ

They are conclusive, thus no misgiving remains,
For those who sow discord and seek not true judgement,

مَا حُورِبَتْ قَطُّ إِلَّا عَادَ مِنْ حَرَبٍ * أَعْدَى الْأَعَادِي إِلَيْهَا مُلْقِيَ السَّلَمِ

They have not been attacked at all, except that the rival party,
Fierce as they may be, returned to them in peace,

رَدَّتْ بَلَاغَتُهَا دَعْوَى مُعَارِضِهَا * رَدَّ الْغَيُورِ يَدَ الْجَانِي عَنِ الْحُرَمِ

Their articulacy repels the claim of their negater,
As the jealous resist the hand of outsiders from their women,

لَهَا مَعَانٍ كَمَوْجِ الْبَحْرِ فِي مَدَدٍ * وَفَوْقَ جَوْهَرِهِ فِي الْحُسْنِ وَالْقِيَمِ

They have meanings like the waves of the sea in abundance,
And beyond their essence in splendour and value,

فَمَا تُعَدُّ وَلَا تُحْصَى عَجَائِبُهَا * وَلَا تُسَامُ عَلَى الْإِكْثَارِ بِالسَّأَمِ

Thus their wonders are neither measured nor tallied,
Nor do they cause exhaustion from increased repetition,

لَمْ تَقْتَرِنْ بِزَمَانٍ وَهْيَ تُخْبِرُنَا
عَنِ الْمَعَادِ وَعَنْ عَادٍ وَعَنْ إِرَمِ
دَامَتْ لَدَيْنَا فَفَاقَتْ كُلَّ مُعْجِزَةٍ
مِنَ النَّبِيِّينَ إِذْ جَاءَتْ وَلَمْ تَدُمِ
مُحَكَّمَاتٌ فَمَا تُبْقِينَ مِنْ شُبَهٍ
لِذِي شِقَاقٍ وَمَا تَبْغِينَ مِنْ حَكَمِ
مَا حُورِبَتْ قَطُّ إِلَّا عَادَ مِنْ حَرَبٍ
أَعْدَى الْأَعَادِي إِلَيْهَا مُلْقِيَ السَّلَمِ
رَدَّتْ بَلَاغَتُهَا دَعْوَى مُعَارِضِهَا
رَدَّ الْغَيُورِ يَدَ الْجَانِي عَنِ الْحَرَمِ
لَهَا مَعَانٍ كَمَوْجِ الْبَحْرِ فِي مَدَدٍ
وَفَوْقَ جَوْهَرِهِ فِي الْحُسْنِ وَالْقِيَمِ
فَمَا تُعَدُّ وَلَا تُحْصَى عَجَائِبُهَا
وَلَا تُسَامُ عَلَى الْإِكْثَارِ بِالسَّأَمِ

قَرَّتْ بِهَا عَيْنُ قَارِئِهَا فَقُلْتُ لَهُ * لَقَدْ ظَفِرْتَ بِحَبْلِ اللهِ فَاعْتَصِمِ

The eyes of their reciter are cooled so I said to him,
You have attained the rope of Allah, so hold tight,

إِنْ تَتْلُهَا خِيفَةً مِنْ حَرِّ نَارِ لَظًى * أَطْفَأْتَ حَرَّ لَظًى مِنْ وِرْدِهَا الشَّبِمِ

If you recite them due to the fear of the intensity of a blazing fire,
They will extinguish its vehement heat through their fragrant litany,

كَأَنَّهَا الْحَوْضُ تَبْيَضُّ الْوُجُوهُ بِهِ * مِنَ الْعُصَاةِ وَقَدْ جَاؤُوهُ كَالْحُمَمِ

As if they are a pond through which brightened faces abound,
Of the disobedient who approach like glowing coals,

وَكَالصِّرَاطِ وَكَالْمِيزَانِ مُعْدِلَةً * فَالْقِسْطُ مِنْ غَيْرِهَا فِي النَّاسِ لَمْ يَقُمِ

Or like the Ṣirāṭ or the scales of justice, for fairness,
From other than it, among people, is not founded,

لَا تَعْجَبَنْ لِحَسُودٍ رَاحَ يُنْكِرُهَا * تَجَاهُلاً وَهُوَ عَيْنُ الْحَاذِقِ الْفَهِمِ

Do not be astonished by the envious who pass the time denying them,
Out of ignorance, while it is the essence of keen understanding,

قَدْ تُنْكِرُ الْعَيْنُ ضَوْءَ الشَّمْسِ مِنْ رَمَدٍ * وَيُنْكِرُ الْفَمُ طَعْمَ الْمَاءِ مِنْ سَقَمٍ

Some eyes may reject the light of the Sun out of deficiencies,
And the mouth may deny the taste of water out of illness."

Al-Shaykh al-Kabīr said, "Whoever recites al-Fātiḥah 70 times a day for seven days while in a state of ablution, then blows into pure water and subsequently drinks it, Allah ﷻ will provide him – through His grace – knowledge and wisdom, purify his heart from corrupt thoughts, and He will confer him a potent memory, by which he will never forget anything that he has heard."

قَرَّتْ بِهَا عَيْنُ قَارِئِهَا فَقُلْتُ لَهُ

لَقَدْ ظَفِرْتَ بِحَبْلِ اللهِ فَاعْتَصِمِ

إِنْ تَتْلُهَا خِيفَةً مِنْ حَرِّ نَارِ لَظَى

أَطْفَأْتَ حَرَّ لَظًى مِنْ وِرْدِهَا الشَّبِمِ

كَأَنَّهَا الْحَوْضُ تَبْيَضُّ الْوُجُوهُ بِهِ

مِنَ الْعُصَاةِ وَقَدْ جَاؤُوهُ كَالْحُمَمِ

وَكَالصِّرَاطِ وَكَالْمِيزَانِ مُعْدِلَةً

فَالْقِسْطُ مِنْ غَيْرِهَا فِي النَّاسِ لَمْ يَقُمِ

لَا تَعْجَبَنْ لِحَسُودٍ رَاحَ يُنْكِرُهَا

تَجَاهُلًا وَهْوَ عَيْنُ الْحَاذِقِ الْفَهِمِ

قَدْ تُنْكِرُ الْعَيْنُ ضَوْءَ الشَّمْسِ مِنْ رَمَدٍ

وَيُنْكِرُ الْفَمُ طَعْمَ الْمَاءِ مِنْ سَقَمِ

قَالَ الشَّيْخُ الْكَبِيرُ: مَنْ قَرَأَ الْفَاتِحَةَ بِالْوُضُوءِ سَبْعَةَ أَيَّامٍ فِي كُلِّ يَوْمٍ سَبْعِينَ مَرَّةً وَنَفَخَ عَلَى مَاءٍ طَاهِرٍ وَشَرِبَهُ يَرْزُقُهُ اللهُ تَعَالَى بِفَضْلِهِ الْعِلْمَ وَالْحِكْمَةَ وَطَهَّرَ قَلْبَهُ مِنَ الْأَفْكَارِ الْفَاسِدَةِ وَجَعَلَهُ ذَكِيّاً لَا يَنْسَى أَبَداً مَا سَمِعَهُ وَقَالَ بَعْضُهُمْ: إِذَا أَدْمَنَ

Others have said, "If a man perseveres in reciting the first four verses of Sūrah al-Baqarah, they will upturn his memory, reinforce his soul, and solidify knowledge in his heart. They also help in attaining gnosis of Allah."

الْمَرْءُ عَلَى قِرَاءَةِ أَوَّلِ سُورَةِ الْبَقَرَةِ (الْآيَاتُ الْأَرْبَعُ) فَهِيَ تَزِيدُ فِي الْحِفْظِ وَتُقَوِّي النَّفْسَ وَتُثَبِّتُ الْعِلْمَ فِي الْقَلْبِ وَتُعِينُ عَلَى مَعْرِفَةِ اللهِ.

Herbs and Foods That Help One to Memorize and Avoid Forgetfulness

It has been upheld, through experimentation, that there are a myriad of special herbs and foods that strengthen memory, invigorate it, help one to memorize, and cure forgetfulness. I will, O honoured reader, list some here:

- Ginger.
- Dates.
- Honey.
- Tea.
- Wild frankincense.
- Carrots.
- Bone marrow.
- Almonds.
- Watercress.
- Rabbit meat.
- Grapes.
- Thyme.
- Olives and olive oil.
- Peach.
- Figs.
- Black raisins.

Al-Zuhrī said, "You should consume honey as it is good for the memory."

أَعْشَابٌ وَأَغْذِيَةٌ تُسَاعِدُ عَلَى الْحِفْظِ وَتَجَنُّبِ النِّسْيَانِ

قَدْ ثَبُتَ بِالتَّجْرِبَةِ أَنَّ هُنَاكَ أَعْشَاباً وَأَغْذِيَةً خَاصَّةً تُقَوِّي الذَّاكِرَةَ وَتُنَشِّطُهَا وَتُسَاعِدُ عَلَى الْحِفْظِ وَتُعَالِجُ النِّسْيَانَ، سَأُقَدِّمُ لَكَ عَزِيزِي الْقَارِئُ بَعْضاً مِنْهَا: الزَّنْجَبِيلُ - التَّمْرُ - الْعَسَلُ - الشَّايُ - اللَّبَانُ الذَّكَرُ (اللَّبَانُ الْبَدَوِيُّ) - الْجَزَرُ - الْمُخُّ - اللَّوْزُ - الْجَرْجِيرُ - الْخِيَارُ - الْعِنَبُ - الزَّعْتَرُ - الزَّيْتُونُ وَزَيْتُهُ - الْخُوخُ - التِّينُ - الزَّبِيبُ الْأَسْوَدُ.

وَقَدْ قَالَ الزُّهْرِيُّ: عَلَيْكَ بِالْعَسَلِ فَإِنَّهُ جَيِّدٌ لِلْحِفْظِ.

Some Compounds That Strengthen One's Retention and Assist in Memorization

- Hot drinks, such as tea, along with seven drops of black seed oil. Such drinks should be consumed on a daily basis on an empty stomach. They may be sweetened with bee's honey or sugar (tried and tested).
- Ginger tea sweetened with sugar. It should be consumed an hour before one's lesson with a copious amount of frankincense, and a drop of its extract.
- Eating raisins in the morning. One Sheikh used to eat 21 raisins every morning, and had an amazing memory. He used to advise their students to do the same.
- A man came to ʿAlī ibn Abī Ṭālib – may Allah ennoble his countenance – and complained to him of suffering from forgetfulness. He said, "You should drink cow's milk, for it instills courage in the heart and dispels forgetfulness."
- Likewise, from that which helps sharpen one's retention capacity is the practice of some people using wild frankincense. They would also counsel others to use it. In sum, they would put a large quantity of it in a container with water, and then leave it overnight until daybreak. Then, they would drink it on an empty stomach.
- From the most beneficial of treatment options is drinking Zamzam water with the intention of strengthening one's memorization. The Prophet ﷺ said, "The water of Zamzam is [effective] for that for which it is drunk." In fact, many of the righteous folk had drunk it with different intentions and Allah fulfilled them.

وَمِنَ الْمُرَكَّبَاتِ الَّتِي تُقَوِّي الذَّاكِرَةَ وَتُسَاعِدُ عَلَى الْحِفْظِ

- مَشْرُوبُ النَّعْنَاعِ كَالشَّاي وَعَلَيْهِ سَبْعُ قَطَرَاتٍ مِنْ زَيْتِ حَبَّةِ الْبَرَكَةِ - الْحَبَّةُ السَّوْدَاءُ - وَيُشْرَبُ عَلَى الرِّيقِ يَوْمِيّاً وَيَكُونُ مُحَلًّى بِعَسَلِ نَحْلٍ أَوْ سُكَّرِ نَبَاتٍ (مُجَرَّبٌ).
- مَشْرُوبُ الزَّنْجَبِيلِ كَالشَّاي مُحَلًّى بِسُكَرِ نَبَاتٍ يُشْرَبُ قَبْلَ الدَّرْسِ بِسَاعَةٍ مَعَ مَضْغِ لَبَّانٍ ذَكَرٍ وَبَلْعِ عُصَارَتِهِ (مُجَرَّبٌ).
- أَكْلُ الزَّبِيبِ فِي الصَّبَاحِ: وَقَدْ كَانَ أَحَدُ الشُّيُوخِ يَأْكُلُ كُلَّ يَوْمٍ فِي الصَّبَاحِ إِحْدَى وَعِشْرِينَ زَبِيبَةً نَظِيفَةً وَكَانَ آيَةً فِي الْحِفْظِ وَكَانَ يُرْشِدُ تَلَامِيذَهُ إِلَى ذَلِكَ.
- وَجَاءَ رَجُلٌ إِلَى عَلِيِّ بْنِ أَبِي طَالِبٍ كَرَّمَ اللهُ وَجْهَهُ فَشَكَا إِلَيْهِ النِّسْيَانَ، فَقَالَ: عَلَيْكَ بِأَلْبَانِ الْبَقَرِ فَإِنَّهُ يُشَجِّعُ الْقَلْبَ وَيُذْهِبُ النِّسْيَانَ.
- كَذَلِكَ مِمَّا يُحَسِّنُ الْحَافِظَةَ مَا كَانَ يَعْمَلُهُ كَثِيرٌ مِنَ النَّاسِ مِنْ اِسْتِعْمَالِ اللَّبَّانِ الْبَدَوِيِّ وَيُوصُونَ بِهِ وَقَدْ كَانُوا يَضَعُونَ كِمِّيَةً مِنْهُ فِي إِنَاءٍ مَعَ مَاءٍ وَيَتْرُكُونَهُ مِنَ اللَّيْلِ إِلَى الصَّبَاحِ وَمِنْ ثَمَّ يَشْرَبُونَهُ عَلَى الرِّيقِ.
- وَمِنَ الْأَدْوِيَةِ النَّافِعَةِ جِدّاً: شُرْبُ مَاءِ زَمْزَمَ بِنِيَّةِ تَقْوِيَةِ الْحِفْظِ، قَالَ النَّبِيُّ صَلَّى اللهُ عَلَيْهِ وَسَلَّمَ «مَاءُ زَمْزَمَ لِمَا شُرِبَ لَه» وَقَدْ شَرِبَهُ عَدَدٌ كَثِيرٌ مِنَ الصَّالِحِينَ بِنِيَّاتٍ مُخْتَلِفَةٍ فَحَقَّقَ اللهُ لَهُمْ ذَلِكَ.

Made in the USA
Middletown, DE
11 August 2024

58550463R00066